In praise of *SHAPERS*

"Work has morphed and you need to shape it. Let this book inspire and guide you."

—Jane Dutton, Professor Emerita, University of Michigan, Co-founder, Center for Positive Organisations

"'Work is no longer just a place, or even a fixed time. How can we make it meaningful rather than just all-consuming? How can we shape our work rather than let it determine how we live? Altman's *SHAPERS* offers answers that are thoughtful, practical and bold."

—Alex Pang, author of *REST*

"An invigorating look at the changing nature of work and how to thrive in the future"

—Edward Vince, Creative Director, Airbnb

"*SHAPERS* is a timely reminder that we are only limited by our beliefs and awareness. When we do the hard work of examining our assumptions, we can co-create the future with a clear mind and open hearts - where our individual and collective potential will flourish."

—Susan Basterfield, Member and Director, Enspiral Foundation and Greaterthan

"With the world shifting under our feet, *SHAPERS* is a frank and honest look at how we can create a more meaningful working life."

—**Joshua Crook, author of *Essays in AI: Automation, Technology and the Future of 9-5 Work***

"The world is changing, and the future of work is up for grabs. *SHAPERS* gives us a blueprint for a future of work that's both sane and humane."

—**David Kadavy, author of *Mind Management, Not Time Management***

'In concise and accessible style, Altman takes us on a multi-disciplinary journey through the sometimes thorny and complex topic of work. An impressive experiment that will force new modes of thought upon you.'

—**Will Stronge, Director of Autonomy and co-author of *Post-Work***

"What constitutes a thriving team, healthy leadership or a successful boss is fundamentally being redefined. Altman invites us into an exploration of the multiple aspects of a work world built around the human spirit and responsiveness to change. This is how we are designed!

—**Samantha Slade, entrepreneur and author of *Going Horizontal***

"What a relief!–you read Altman's *SHAPERS* and realize that, yes, anyone can bend with the waves. This is less a book about the changing face of work (though it surely is that also) and more a guide to how to be flexible, resourceful, and graceful as a genuine maker of your own path. In jazzy, often galloping prose, Altman shows us how to be free spirits–and why living this way matters."
—Adrew Taggart, founder, Askole and author of *Total Work*

SHAPERS

SHAPERS

REINVENT THE WAY YOU WORK
AND CHANGE THE FUTURE

JONAS ALTMAN

WILEY

This edition first published 2020

Copyright © 2020 by Jonas Altman. All rights reserved.

Registered office

John Wiley & Sons Ltd, The Atrium, Southern Gate, Chichester, West Sussex, PO19 8SQ, United Kingdom

For details of our global editorial offices, for customer services and for information about how to apply for permission to reuse the copyright material in this book please see our website at www.wiley.com.

Wiley publishes in a variety of print and electronic formats and by print-on-demand. Some material included with standard print versions of this book may not be included in e-books or in print-on-demand. If this book refers to media such as a CD or DVD that is not included in the version you purchased, you may download this material at http://booksupport.wiley.com. For more information about Wiley products, visit www.wiley.com.

Designations used by companies to distinguish their products are often claimed as trademarks. All brand names and product names used in this book are trade names, service marks, trademarks or registered trademarks of their respective owners. The publisher is not associated with any product or vendor mentioned in this book.

Library of Congress Cataloging-in-Publication Data is Available:

ISBN 9781119659044 (hardback)
ISBN 9781119658931 (ePDF)
ISBN 9781119658900 (ePub)

Cover Design: Luiz Ferraz Junior

Set in 11.5/18pt MinionPro by SPi Global, Chennai, India

Printed and bound by CPI Group (UK) ltd, Croydon, CR0 4YY

10 9 8 7 6 5 4 3 2 1

CONTENTS

CONTENTS

What you do makes a difference, and you have to decide what kind of difference you want to make.

—Jane Goodall

INTRODUCTION: A WATERSHED MOMENT

Manny likes fish tacos. I mean, he really, *really* likes them. We plunk down in red folding chairs at opposite ends of a table at his favourite local taco stand, and Manny sets to work dressing a trio of mahi-mahi tacos. A little onion. A sliver of avocado. A pinch of cilantro. A generous squeeze of fresh lime. With such meticulous, almost ritualistic care, it's a miracle he ever finishes prepping them. I'm already two bites into my second *al pastor* before, finally, Manny sports a wide-ass grin and takes a bite.

Manny is a shaper, *literally*–this is what people who make surfboards by hand are called. His work is as precise as it is passionate, rooted in tradition and as innovative as hell, with every board a unique reflection of his personality. It's an unconventional career choice and, to Manny, it's more than a profession; it's his calling. Challenging. Meaningful. Infinitely fulfilling.

He's also a shaper in the way he shows up in his community, supports independent businesses, and leads environmental initiatives. The mindset of a shaper is about connecting your work with your *self*. As we'll come to understand, it requires self-awareness, self-belief, and continual growth.

I met Manny at the turn of the century while living in San Francisco. Years later, I heard he'd fallen off the face of the earth. So on a whim, I decided to pay him a visit to see if indeed he had. Turns out he was living in Leucadia, a seductive town north of San Diego. This curious human had created one hell of a colourful life for himself. His positive energy was contagious and I wanted what he was having.

Born Manuel Caro to Filipino parents, Manny and his family moved from Laos to southern California when he was two. As a kid, he'd spend his early mornings riding waves and the rest of the day playing the dutiful son, doing his chores and finishing his homework. But then Manny's dad up and left, and at just fourteen, the boy had to grow up fast. 'I [learned] how to use a screwdriver and fix things because no one else was there to do it,' he explains, taking a swig of fizzy water.

He set his sights on becoming a marine biologist but soon found out how much he sucked at calculus. So he abandoned marine science and opted to study anthropology; humans would have to make do over sea-life. With his mom and younger sister in tow, Manny's plan was to keep his head down, work hard, and follow a familiar script: study → college → job → success. However, life sometimes has other plans for us, and Manny's was no exception. None of it, he recounts between bites, went according to script.

As the dot-com bubble burst and sent its devastating effects rippling throughout the country, Manny took a soul-sapping retail job–anything to pay the bills–and shacked up in a shed in a rough part of Oakland, California. Things were pretty dismal, but Manny stuck to his (now slightly modified) plan: keep your head down, work hard, and find a way forward when you can. And in the meantime, he surfed.

Manny had gotten used to the looks he'd get from the other surfers. A vivacious Latin soul housed inside a geeky 5′5 Filipino body, Manny was a far cry from the typical beach-blond dudes parked in the tiny beach lot in Pacifica, a town just south of San Francisco. His board stood out too. While the other guys rocked the popular three-finned thrusters, Manny guarded a bizarre-looking quad fish surfboard. As the name suggests, the quad fish has four fins and a tail that resembles a chirpy carp about to chow down on dinner. You could say the look was, well, *whack*, but it suited Manny just swimmingly. And besides, the heckling would usually stop as soon as he caught his first wave.

See, Manny's odd-looking board had a big advantage in that it was super fast. And Manny was a crackerjack surfer. He gracefully carved his turns on the waves, turning the heads of every onlooker on the beach as he did. When it came time to pack it up and head back to the parking lot, Manny would invariably get stopped by a sea-sprayed bro. 'Hey, can I see that thing?' the onetime mocker now turned gawker would ask. Such interactions would prove formative in more ways than one.

'It occurred to me at that moment that the rest of my life isn't going to be determined by other people's formulas,' Manny recalls of the experience. 'I'm going to determine my own formula—because nothing else is really going to work.' Trusting his instincts, Manny became the steward to his gifts.

*   *   *

Alongside his boisterous laugh, that funny *quad fish* from the parking lot has become his signature design. Manny had tapped into the thing that he needed to be doing in this life. He didn't mind one bit that I was waiting (and salivating) while he calmly doctored up that taco. He had ceased conforming to what the world wanted him to be and began bopping to his own beat.

Shapers adhere to a craftsman-like culture. If you're a shaper, you put your stamp on your work. You earn your stripes. You sync with a rhythm of life that lights you up. At times, work may be a frightening obstacle (and obsession), but shapers move through adversity with temperament and tenacity. A determination to continually improve and evolve. A willingness to experiment and learn from mistakes. To create on the fly. To work fluidly. To persevere and be patient in equal measure. To unwaveringly nourish the soul.

A shaper is someone who becomes energised by work. The way they work provides for the highest expression of self. They lead deeper and more fulfilling lives because what they do everyday serves them and the greater good.

If it sounds like I'm talking about more than handcrafting surfboards, I am. Now, more than ever, the professional working world needs a bit of the shaper shimmer.

I should know, after years of trying to run a business with the wrong partner, in the wrong industry and in the wrong way– I burned out. So I up and left and went back to school to study design and to figure out where I went wrong. Or perhaps why I went wrong. It turned out that my workaholism was a container for my fear of failure. Instead of working smart and with purpose, I just kept my head down and toiled away harder.

I discovered that my approach to work was crushing my spirit so I swapped it for one that helped me come alive. I began to see that my vitality would only come when I gave into my curiosity and creativity. I realised that I needed to rest and reassess so that I could show up for others as my best self. Over time I was able to earn a living by doing what fuels me–learning, teaching, and helping.

I know too that I'm no exception–because every day I work with people who use the strategies in this book to transform how they work and discover meaning. I've witnessed these approaches succeed time and again. Producing over posturing. Empowering over embittering. Asking over telling. Giving over taking. Leaning in rather than opting out.

It's no secret that we're facing an unprecedented crisis in work: Gallup polls regularly report that the majority of the working world is not engaged in what they do. The contributors to this crisis are a smorgasbord of realities, including the growing financial divide, a widening skills gap, unemployment, precarious work, diversity issues, and algorithms and automation that keep gobbling up jobs. Along with climate change, the crisis of work is one of the biggest challenges we face. Indeed, the two are inextricably linked. The good news is that there are people and companies already making work a whole lot better.

And so we find ourselves at a watershed moment. Now is an extraordinary time in which we can indulge the human spirit and our impulse to do the work that matters. Instead of clinging to age-old attitudes, we have a ripe opportunity to reimagine work and our place in it. We have an unprecedented chance to renew ourselves in the work we do.

Margaret Mead was a shaper. So too was Alvin Toffler. Yvon Chouinard is a shaper as is Marie Forleo. And a tide of burgeoning shapers are rushing in. They're eager to find meaning in their work and reinvent our organisations. What's crucial now are the decisions we make going forward and whether we can let go of the structures, systems, and practices of a bygone era and come together to do the work our world needs.

The future of work is about the meaning you discover. It's about the shape that we collectively give it. That's what we're here to explore in this book. Drawing from hundreds of interviews, we'll apply anecdotes from CEOs, organisational designers, social psychologists, workplace strategists, marketing gurus, design ninjas, startup entrepreneurs, restless raconteurs, culture geeks, creative freaks, and a plethora of other trailblazers all helping to shape the future of work. We'll dive inside companies like Netflix, Squarespace, LEGO, and Patagonia to see how they cultivate resilient work cultures. We'll see precisely how shapers fuel themselves by what they do every day and how you can do the same.

In Part One, we'll explore the history of work and how we find ourselves at this watershed moment. In Part Two, we'll look at the organisations and people that are pioneering work in new and exciting ways. And since there are many possible futures, in Part Three, we'll consider the principles that can help you navigate your way to a preferable one.

Whether you're in the C-suite or the front line, work remotely or in an office–the ideas, lessons, and tools presented in these pages are for you to adopt as you see fit. Pick, mix, experiment, and run with whatever works best for you. We all have different approaches to work, and each one of us can find those opportunities for growth. We can all evolve. My invitation is for you to thoughtfully shape and regularly refine the ways you work.

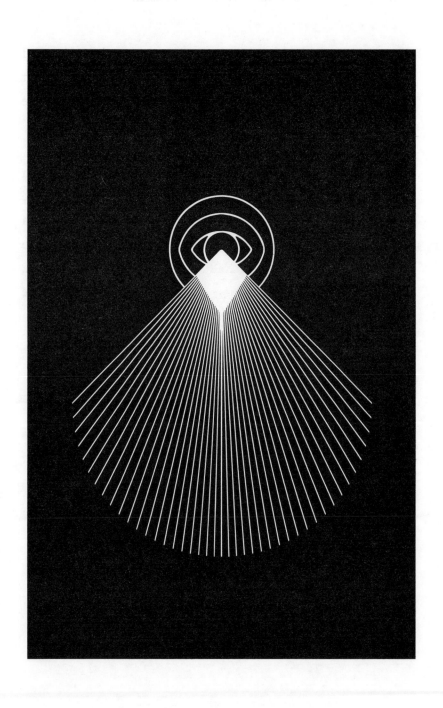

PART I

MEANING AND THE NATURE OF WORK

Everything can be taken from a man but one thing: the last of the human freedoms–to choose one's attitude in any given set of circumstances, to choose one's own way.

—Viktor Frankl

The nature of work is quickly changing so that more of us can find meaning in what we do. And given the opportunity, it's absolutely imperative that we search for work that lights us up. At this watershed moment, with massive disengagement and a system of work that is broken–we can embrace the drive we all have within. As shapers we pursue our vision for fulfilling work because it impacts every aspect of our lives and the lives of those around us.

CHAPTER 1

THE MAGIC OF MEANING

Work is now a practice through which we search for meaning to help shape a colourful life. The choice we have is to move beyond ourselves and connect with something larger. This deep sense of commitment and purpose is non-negotiable and is what gives shapers their shimmer.

Last I checked, they don't stock bottles of happiness on store shelves. (OK, depending on where you shop and what's in the bottle, perhaps they do.) Instead, the shelves are lined with books about the *pursuit* of happiness. If you want to learn how to find your bliss, chase down the things that spark joy, and untether your soul, there's no shortage of authors and teachers who are glad to point the way in exchange for a handful of your dollars. What you don't see lining the walls of bookstores and the splash pages of your go-to guru is the promise of *keeping* happiness once you have it. It's a promise nobody—at least, nobody honest–is going to make.

Happiness is fleeting. It comes and goes, flexes and flops, rises and pops. A double-scoop ice-cream cone might fall to the floor or melt divinely in your mouth, but whichever way, it's gone and so is the momentary happiness it brought. And that makes happiness a moving target and, therefore, a crappy career goal.

Shapers know that happiness is perpetually in flux and hinges upon getting what you want, or at least getting what you think you want at various times. And it's fleeting. It comes and goes, flexes and flops, rises and pops. A double-scoop ice-cream cone might fall to the floor or melt divinely in your mouth; but either way it's gone and so is the momentary happiness it brought. And that makes happiness a moving target and, therefore, a crappy career goal.

Meaning, a close cousin to happiness, is much more astute. The magic of meaning is that it persists through time. We can move to and from meaning again and again because it's not a destination to which we hope to arrive–but discursively comes from what we give our attention and energy to. Often it's when we connect with something larger than ourselves that meaning makes a cameo.

Meaning is nuanced and textured. It's subjective. It's a choice that emerges from those things to which we ascribe significance. But it's slippery as hell because it's not always clear what those things are at any given time. It could be pinned on someone, something, or some place. When felt, when lived–meaning spirals into our soul and provides for an expansive sense of self. It helps connect the once seemingly unconnected through time.

Meaning matters because it lets us show up in the world as we were meant to be. It propels our inner drive. It gives us energy. It provides the colour to our lives. We need meaning both for the will to live and the ability to grow.

Since most have abandoned religion in favour of work in the secular West, we now seek an enduring sense of purpose not from the house of God but the church of work. The largest religious group in the U.S.A is, you guessed it, 'non-believers.' We've supplanted the altar with the office, the Bible with the smartphone, and come to expect righteous Sundays every damn day.

We're searching for 'daily meaning as well as daily bread,' wrote broadcaster Studs Terkel about work. It's in the spiritual practice of work where the hunt for self-actualisation and even transcendence now takes place. And for something to hold meaning, it must be seen as valuable in the eyes of the beholder, to our culture, or both. For shapers, this search is a compulsion–they're always getting closer.

In order to boost our chances of finding and sustaining meaning–we need to *stop* divorcing ourselves from our work. Basta! Instead, we should inject ourselves quirks and all, into what we do. For shapers this is a heartfelt obligation. It's how they make their best contribution to the world. And then like a swell in the ocean, that unmistakable feeling of meaning rushes in.

To be certain, we can often confuse urgency with meaning. When the pressure is so heavy and the exigency so real, we attribute what we're experiencing as supremely significant. It may be in the face of adversity or confronting our fatality that might expedite a sense meaning, but none of these are necessary conditions. All that's required is the ability to choose.

When you believe in your uniqueness, you stop trying to fit a mould; you move closer to becoming your truest self. You cater to your impulse to create. 'If happiness is about getting what you want, it appears that meaningfulness is about doing things that express yourself,' reveals social psychologist Roy Baumeister. For a shaper, this is the ultimate freedom *and* responsibility.

It may be paradoxical, but shapers understand that finding meaning typically appears when we're not looking for it. By plunging into something bigger than ourselves, setting aside our 'convulsive little egos' as the father of American psychology, William James would put it, meaning can gently bubble up. For example, I studied digital marketing to go into the music business, and lo and behold, I bumped into the love of my life.

Meaning ensues from a process of discovery and defeat. During the ups and the downs, turning points, and in between all the gnarly waves that life brings, shapers show up wholeheartedly in the present. They enjoy the fruits of their labour as well as the process, the sweat, and the struggle. This unyielding commitment to a purpose is what gives shapers their shimmer.

Shapers begin with their *why,* and then figure out the *how.* Their interiority let's them create meaning time and again. Their self-efficacy let's them shun the negative self-talk and spiral upwards. They feel part of something larger than themselves. There is sacrifice, yes. Settling, no.

DUTY AND LUXURY

In a large international study of the most meaningful things in life, work was mentioned 44% of the time, ranking second only to family. Of course, if we poll different people at different stages in their life, and from across different cultures—we're bound to get different results. But for many people, work will always be their darling.

One of the most pervasive facets of Japanese work culture is the distinct pride they take in their work. The Japanese call this *shokunin*; a term once reserved for the domain of craftspeople, today it's seeping into many aspects of Japanese working life with the implicit duty to perform at one's best. Japanese sculptor Toshio Odate explains:

> The Japanese word shokunin is defined by both Japanese and Japanese-English dictionaries as 'craftsman' or 'artisan,' but such a literal description does not fully express the deeper meaning. The Japanese apprentice is taught that shokunin means not only having technical skills, but also implies an attitude and social consciousness .... The shokunin has a social obligation to work his or her best for the general welfare of the people. This obligation is both spiritual and material, in that no matter what, the shokunin's responsibility is to fulfil the requirement.

Irrespective of who it is or what responsibility they may be fulfilling, many Japanese workers have pep in their step. There are several reasons for this phenomenon, but two reasons stand out. The first boils down to Japan as an island country. Just a bit bigger geographically than Great Britain, their respective island mentalities couldn't be further apart. In Japan, there is a cultural conformity to give everything you got to whatever it is you do. This 'we're all in this together' sentiment is reinforced by strict legislation. In other words, if an investment banker in the City of London shits the bed on a deal, he gets fired, but the same banker in Tokyo simply gets transferred to Osaka.

The second reason has to do with family. The drive for this kind of conscientious behaviour in Japanese workers stems from deep-seated family bonds. It's precisely why out of all the businesses worldwide that have been around for over 100 years, 90% are Japanese. And they all keep it tight with fewer than 300 employees. Instead of striving to grow faster, they endure because they endeavour to grow better.

Whether in or outside of work, what spurs us to integrate is evolution itself. More folks could take a cue from the Japanese where good work, good business, and good citizenry for that matter, envelop a deep personal commitment to making your best contribution.

Take Simon Mhanna for example. Emigrating from Lebanon to Canada, Mhanna has swiftly become a national design leader. The quintessential shaper wakes up each day knowing he's flexing his chance to serve. 'I worked hard to find opportunities that align with my passion and that allow me to fulfil my purpose. I show up true to myself, my feelings, and my beliefs–which makes it hard for me to separate the self from the work,' he explains. It's his authentic intention and sense of self that enables Mhanna to deeply connect with his work.

By knowing what you value and how you are valued, you can blend yourself into your work. That feeling that you're making a real difference is unmistakable. And when you're a part of something larger than yourself, meaning is bound to come.

LOVE AND WORK

We glorify love and work and indeed the two are forever enmeshed in an intricate dance. 'They are also locked in mortal combat,' claims philosopher Alain de Botton. Like love, work is a practice–a daily operation that, over time, shapes the fabric of our lives.

This business of finding fulfilling work is no easy feat. With less replication, stability, and certainty, we've gained more choice in work, but we've also encountered a sweeping sense of self-doubt.

Never has the burden on the self been so damn heavy. Amidst more uncertainty, we yearn for a sense of control often found by succumbing to that taunting voice in our heads to do more. But we don't need to control everything to get a good outcome.

We have to take time for ourselves to quieten the inner critic, manage our anxiety, and minimise our stress. I'm exhausted just thinking about it, let alone writing about it. This approach all adds up to a thick layer of emotional labour that's rarely talked about or valued, much less quantified or even seen.

Meaning, if and when it shows up, can be beautifully random and randomly beautiful. And work, whether or not we like it, is a popular laboratory for making meaning. Like love, we throw ourselves into it. We encounter it. We fall into it. Sometimes we do so as a diversion from other facets of our lives. Other times we do so to move just that bit closer to our dreams. And in some instances, we do both.

Is it any wonder, then, that we feel stifled when we can't see ourselves making progress in work? That we feel disillusioned when the career ladder has collapsed and our attempts to impact our communities and leave a mark on the world has become more challenging? Work progression now resembles a labyrinth, and we're left feeling stunted as the result. This topsy-turvy trajectory gets frustrating, even infuriating. But shapers find that it's precisely this psychologically uncomfortable feeling that leads to meaningful change.

These times where things don't quite go as well as expected, can, if we're open to it, lead to the most interesting of new horizons. We have an opportunity to nurture our talent, fuel our interest, and make an even bigger impact in the world. The only question is whether we're ready to do so.

CHAPTER 2
A SHORT HISTORY OF WORK

Throughout history, work was mostly miserable with little if any room for self-expression. As punishment for the Original sin, drudgery was a potential stairway to heaven. Modern management commands productivity and progress while our attitudes towards work becomes bound to time on the clock. With the advent of the Internet, we are untethered from our desk and provided with endless opportunities to express ourselves. We're now set on giving life to the multitude of selves within us.

The port of Athens, with its colourful walks of life, was the perfect backdrop to waxing lyrical on the best way to live. Plato and his gang (Socrates, Glaucon, and co.) would cruise the buzzing streets of Piraeus intoxicated by the sights and sea. It was in this serene setting that Plato began shaping the world's most important philosophical work.

Platonic idealism (alongside the ancient Greek philosophies) was instrumental in giving rise to democracy and laying the bedrock of modern Western civilisation. 'There will be no end to the troubles of states, or of humanity itself, till philosophers become kings in this world, or till those we now call kings and rulers really and truly become philosophers,' is one of his finer lines.

In Plato's Republic, the ideal state is divided into three distinct classes: the Producers, who provide material and functional needs; the Auxiliaries, who defend the state; and the Guardians, who govern it. Justice is maintained when every person within a respective class performs his or her proper function in society.

For a long time, I was hung up on a philosopher who lived some 2400 years ago proclaiming the best way for everyone to live, and in particular how I should live. Oh, the gall to speak of the desires of my soul and then exclude them from expression! Admittedly those were different times and I've grossly oversimplified things.

Still, it would be fun to see the expression on Plato's face were he dropped into a present-day Shibuya Crossing in Tokyo. Gobsmacked! He rubs his eyes repeatedly, not from the neon lights (although those nearly blind him) but from how technology and mankind move in unison together. With his jaw dropped well below his chiton, we could explain that the world is connected through a vast wired network, that large containers whisk us through the sky high above oceans, and from time to time we travel to other bodies in the galaxy.

Or better yet, if we could travel back in time to Piraeus circa 380 BC and demonstrate our progress as a civilisation. As writer Tom Streithorst hints, 'With an AK-47, a home brewing kit, or a battery-powered vibrator, startled [onlookers] would worship at our feet.' Imagine still yet, if we were to explain that we've designed machines that actually learn. They can play, paint, sing, write, dance, see, drive, fly and so much more—abiding by whatever program we set. Dearest Plato, the cherished functions of the soul are now augmented by mechanical minds that we've designed in our image.

And technological advancements have shaped and continue to transform work in unimaginable ways. We've even come up with a snazzy name for this era: the Fourth Industrial Revolution. These super-intelligent instruments are integral to our lives and when used, not abused, can make our work culture oh so colourful.

OUR VALUES AT WORK

This is by no means a detailed summation of the history of work. It's purposefully brief so that we may get quicker to the heart of the matter. You will notice the terms *work* and *job* used liberally. While a conception of both can be housed under the efforts to procure the means of survival, I use *work* much more expansively. The discerning qualities of each are as follows:

Job: compensated or waged activities formally provided to an employer. The market determines financial compensation. Features a psychological contract and a veil of security.

Work: deliberate activities engaged to achieve a goal of subjective significance. May or may not be compensated. A contract is not necessary, only the requisite motivation and resilience to accomplish something for the self and the greater good.

The concept of work continues to mutate and our attitudes are still playing catch up. Sometimes we can't see the bigger picture. The issue is not what role the individual should play in society. But it's to do with approaches to, and beliefs about, work. What constitutes work? What do we value? And why are so many of us dissatisfied in the work we do?

The word for work in Greek is Ponos. It originates from the Latin poena, meaning sorrow. The ancient Greeks, as well as the Hebrews and medieval Christians, viewed work as a curse. At its base, work was pain and drudgery. It was the divine punishment for man's original sin and my God were we meant to atone for it.

As a religious responsibility, work allowed little room for self-expression. The 'do what you love' mantra touted by life hackers and career advice columnists today would be extremely suspect. The value that was found in work came irrespective of the extrinsic reward. You worked in exchange for a non-stop first-class ticket to heaven. Without the benefit of contemplation or control, acceptance of one's duty was pretty palatable.

In the 16th century, with the protestant work ethic exalted by Martin Luther, the concept of work emerged as a moral duty. The sacrifice of a hard day's work meant you were helping humanity progress. Wealth creation and accumulation was no longer a vice or an advantage–it was your sweet obligation.

The force that produced this duty was the 'Creed associated with the name Calvin. Capitalism was the social counterpart of Calvinist theology,' wrote economic historian R. H. Tawney. Work was not only for economic means but also as a spiritual end. Similarly today, in the spirit of capitalism and economic self-interest, we seek salvation through an 'orgy of materialism'.

When married to religion, the spirit of hard work was evident in even the most mundane professions. Endless toil could be justified because God, well, blessed it didn't he? With the industrial revolution of the 18th century came a change in our work ethic: a myopic focus on the returns for the individual. The meaning of work veered away from internal motivations to external rewards. Productivity and pay became the principal agenda of work.

Over time, these industrial-age attitudes were baked like layers of lasagna into our organisations. Cemented further by Adam Smith's 'Wealth of Nations', our division of labour meant breaking work down into the smallest, most mundane activities so as to produce more widgets faster. Smith believed that fundamentally people were lazy gits. He thought that so long as you paid someone a decent wage, it didn't really matter what job they performed. Dangling carrots would induce workers to work harder.

Individual control over the techniques and quantity of personal production began to fade with the rise of automation. The race against the machines began. If you worked in agriculture or crafts, you might advance upward in society. Otherwise, you were aware that your job was expendable and soon to be performed by a machine. This is indeed a conundrum in which many of today's Uber drivers may find themselves.

When Frederick Winslow Taylor, the first management consultant, snagged the baton from Smith, the *batching* of work found its soulmate in a new management practice. Taylorism began with the question, 'How many tonnes of pig iron bars can a worker load onto a railcar in one working day?' Its 'scientific management' involved managers closely controlling workers with the objective of maximising efficiency, consistency, predictability, and productivity.

Just think of the Ford Motor Assembly Line. No doubt Henry Ford chose black for the Model T Classic simply because this colour dried the fastest and would trim production time.

Organisations then competed for control over finite resources like coal and iron. Since everything was vertically integrated, business success meant outmaneuvering the competition while labourers were reduced to cogs in the machine.

This period also gave birth to the *short-time movement;* the 8-hour workday and 40-hour workweek that are familiar benchmarks today. While temporarily shortened to 30-hour weeks during the Great Depression in America, after World War II it snapped right back. It lent well into a straight shot of overtime, wage increases, and benefits still keenly protected.

Economist John Maynard Keynes, who envisaged we'd work a 15-hour work week, would certainly be scratching his head. Science and compound interest have hardly led the masses to live in leisure–in the process losing the chance to 'Live wisely and agreeably and well'. While we have made tremendous progress, our enhanced productivity has resulted in the insatiable desires and relentless consumerism which comprise our modern collective psyche.

WORK AS AN EXPRESSION NOT A PLACE

With the advent of the microchip in the 1970s and acceleration of economic globalisation in the 1980s, work slowly became unhinged from geographical limitations. With a strong WiFi connection it became easier to pool resources from any capable worker anywhere. Peter Drucker's knowledge worker entered his or her heyday and companies began duking it out to retain their greatest asset: their people. The war for talent continues today.

The tools and practices of knowledge management blossomed in the 1990s to support the new wave of workers. Futurist and early shaper, Alvin Toffler had long imagined a knowledge economy that would require a system for workers to create, process, and boost their knowledge–because, for the first time ever, we would own the 'technology of consciousness'.

Information would also need to be managed and shared between colleagues. Organisational theorist Ikujiro Nonaka, another pioneer shaper, wanted to help managers appreciate how knowledge– the fuel for innovation–could be leveraged. He viewed the organisation as an organism that requires constant renewal; and knowledge workers as the designated change agents.

Indeed, the information economy is growing and the wave of knowledge workers continues to swell higher. To that end, most of the ideas in this book are focused on the knowledge economy and those who consistently gather, process, and distribute information. There is becoming less need to trek to, and suffer in, a spirit-sapping office. The most important weapon for businesses today is the ability to empower their workers. Shapers want to be *challenged* like a superhero, not confined to a cage like a zoo animal. And if the firm fails to provide us with what we crave, we'll go elsewhere or simply fuel ourselves.

In the developed world we are fortunate to have plenty of opportunities to entertain such aspirations. Many, both inside and outside of advanced economies, don't have the same good fortune. A whopping 40% of Americans are 'liquid asset poor', or–in plain English–just one paycheck away from poverty.

> The most important weapon for businesses today is the ability to empower their workers. Shapers want to be challenged like a superhero, not confined to a cage like a zoo animal.

Still we lay about daydreaming about the endless ways we might express ourselves, whether it be as a coffee connoisseur, YouTube sensation, kitesurfing pro, or venture capitalist. The choice has become paradoxical. As our expectations for self-expression grow, we may be left deflated and our lofty dreams remain unfulfilled. We long to give life to any or all of our multitudinous selves. Peeling back another layer of the onion reveals that our current crisis of work is also a psychological one.

Of course, things will appear to have different shades to different people depending on their point of view. Flexible work often misconstrued as 'working from home', is all about choice. Seasoned flex workers weave their careers in a way that best suits their talents, skills, and attitude. Sociologist Sebastian Pranz writes:

> They exploit the full potential of their social networks and profit from the fact that, both spatially and mentally, they are now only loosely connected to a company. Flexible work creates a certain culture that has shifted from the structural conditions of job markets to the self-identification of the company and from there it gradually seeps into the worldviews of the workers and their families. 'New capitalism' becomes a new way for us to think about ourselves, our work and our life.

For centuries, wage labour has commanded that we get our kicks elsewhere. Human flourishing has played second fiddle to the capitalist agenda. But shapers yearn to do work that pays by fulfilling the soul. And now, at last, shapers are able to direct their own energies and remove the shackles that restricted the possibility for meaningful work.

CHAPTER 3

EMPLOYEE DISENGAGEMENT EPIDEMIC

The majority of workers are presently disengaged at work. They feel they're not making meaningful progress and not cognitively or emotionally connecting to their work or workplace. This results in an unprecedented loss of productivity as well as a general malaise. This contagion takes a physical and mental toll on workers that can lead to burnout, depression, and other debilitating conditions.

I heard a story about an employee who scripted his own piece of software. The bizarre thing is that its sole function was to make it appear to onlookers as if he were toiling away on his computer, when in fact he was busy exchanging hot tamale recipes (or something equally absurd). By no means is he alone–much of the working world would rather do something, almost anything else for that matter, other than their jobs.

In work that is routine and low discretion, gleaning a profound sense of purpose is rare. But nearly half of Americans now work in non-routine, cognitively demanding jobs. The opportunity to find meaning in work has never been more ripe.

And for those who have been coasting along in aimless work, the mere notion that they might find fulfilment can lead to an existential crisis. They must face the stark reality that their jobs, as anthropologist David Graeber puts it, could be bullshit.

A bullshit job is one in which the employee can honestly admit their job is pointless. Or in other words, if the job were to disappear it wouldn't make a difference. Graeber makes the case that for many of these kinds of jobs, should they vanish, the world would become an even better place. Clerical workers, administrators, PR consultants, telemarketers, and middle managers are frequently cited roles.

Indeed, some may perform a pointless job but still find it provides a sense of meaning. At its most rudimentary, they may extract purpose in being able to provide for themselves and their family. And if they're given the freedom to act responsibly, they might even transform their job so it has utility. Still others might actually possess meaningful work but be in the odd frame of mind where they just don't feel it.

A MONDAY THROUGH FRIDAY SORT OF DYING

At the time of writing, Gallup reports that a whopping 85% of the world's 1 billion full-time employees are not engaged in their work. And this figure has been roughly the same since Gallup began monitoring engagement in the workplace at the turn of this century. Employee disengagement is a global epidemic.

When more than 8 out of every 10 workers endure, or possibly even suffer, a *Monday through Friday sort of dying*, something has to give. In the USA particularly, employee disengagement is appalling. In a 2018 Gallup report, only 34% of employees said they were engaged in their jobs. The majority, then, are disengaged, which means they are not cognitively and emotionally connected to their work or workplace. Instead of just scripting dodgy software to mask their work from time to time, they repeatedly arrive at work aiming to do the least amount they can get away with. There's nothing distinctively unusual about *not working* at work.

Still worse are the 13% of Americans who are 'actively disengaged'. This means that employees are pent-up inside and *acting out* on their resentment. They are often bitter because they feel their needs are being ignored. Deemed to be toxic, they undermine the work of their engaged colleagues. Their venom is contagious and can quickly spread throughout their team, the company floor, and even the entire organisation.

And this is just the tip of the iceberg. In one French study, a CEO said that 19% of his workers were so disengaged that they were planning to sabotage the organisation–they disliked it that much (they didn't act for fear of losing their jobs).

Indeed, emotional states play a part in every facet of our working lives–from what we contribute through to how we might feel a sense of belonging. The emotions of one worker can emanate outwards in all directions, affecting everything and everyone in their path. The side effects of feeling disengaged include apathy, boredom, lack of purpose, and incompetence. You bet this can result in a serious case of the Mondays.

Put into a financial context, the estimated savings from firing (or avoiding the hiring of a toxic employee) is $12,489. This figure does not include other potential costs such as litigation and associated burdens like time away in court, headhunter fees, and lower employee morale. And disengaged workers (often found to have traces of toxicity) cost the American economy alone $350 billion per year in lost productivity. This works out to $1000 for every US citizen. Worldwide, unmotivated workers have spurred decades of steady decline in productivity measured as global GDP per capita.

The effects of disengaged workers don't stop at shitty company performance, productivity, or profit.

Engaged workers are less likely to have accidents, take sick days, make mistakes, behave badly with co-workers and family, burnout, or suffer from depression than their disengaged counterparts. Oh yes, and engaged workers often enjoy their work for its own reward too.

The malaise of the modern worker will not be cured in one fell swoop. It will happen through itsy bitsy nudges in behaviour. Take email for starters. On average, 77% of workers surveyed in the UK claim that a productive day is 'clearing their email' and 40% say that four or more hours of 'doing email' is a good day's work.

The problem does not rest in the technology itself, but in the beliefs about its benefits. The application of electronic mail can be a lazy way out–crippling work instead of advancing it. Boosting team performance and institutionalising healthy behaviour starts with the individual. Changing a nasty email habit, or ceasing to trash-talk colleagues behind their back for that matter, means reshaping both mindsets and habits. And this then seeps into collective behaviour and organisational culture.

FEELING PROGRESS

The biggest stoke in work is whether you believe you're making headway in purposeful work. 'Of all the events that engage people at work, the single most important–by far–is simply making progress in meaningful work,' explains Harvard business professor, Teresa Amabile. Known as the progress principle, it's this type of inner drive that propels shapers to do their best work.

High on the list of making progress in work is gaining a sense of appreciation to keep you motivated. We all want validation, and the best way to get it is by gaining positive (and constructive) feedback from others. When co-workers and collaborators recognise and appreciate your contribution, it can help keep your work mojo firing. We've gotten accustomed to workplace recognition in the form of better salaries, bigger offices, and badass job titles, when really it's this sense of being appreciated that often makes all the difference.

Finding and sustaining meaning in work is a deeply personal affair that starts with you. Shapers know this and continually challenge themselves to sense and respond to what they need to connect to their purpose.

Perhaps the overlooked reason for rampant disengagement at work is simply to do with narrative fallacies. For many folks, those stories that once conjured up anxiety and dread might soon be seen as existential openings. It's only when we all rethink work, and our place in it, that we'll arrive at the root of the problem.

It's through creative expression, guidance, support, experimentation, and a myriad of other avenues that we pursue the work that matters. And along the way—we help ourselves and others to rise up.

CHAPTER 4

INHUMANE RESOURCES

People aren't resources to be managed. Pioneering organisations know this and thus set out to inspire and challenge their talent with a compelling purpose. Because when workers have fertile ground–they'll endeavour to learn, share, and create in order to make their best contribution.

What started out as a blogging platform in the dorm room of founder Anthony Casalena has quietly morphed into one of New York's top places to work. His company, Squarespace, helps anyone create beautiful functional websites. The business's special sauce includes a space where employees have the freedom to do their life's best work. This is achieved by cultivating a culture that is open, supportive, and—spoiler alert—highly creative. Squarespace is the poster child for how a compelling purpose can turn any worker into an evangelist.

Squarespace's headquarters is a destination to which employees flock to work, learn, share, create, and hangout. Because they love being there, employees commute to the office when they could just as easily work from home. Staff are not seen as resources to be managed, but as humans to be challenged.

INVESTING IN PEOPLE

When traditional labour-oriented jobs gave way to knowledge-based ones, most corporations failed to upgrade their recruitment incentives. Some started to individualise rewards, giving each employee an opportunity to tailor a benefits package. But few reoriented towards the seismic shift in the market. Today, shapers have learned that giving employees control and empowering them so that meaning might ensue is the name of the game. Third-wave workers 'Seek meaning along with financial reward', declared Alvin Toffler over 40 years ago. Many HR departments are just slow to read the memo–still trying to lure employees with pay and perks (and that veil of security).

Trailblazing organisations like Squarespace and Patagonia have high retention rates because they *inspire* and *challenge* their people. While less pedantic about contractual distinctions, these companies appreciate that the competition for talent has merely evolved into an endless game of Tetris. They've abandoned mass synchronisation in favour of agility that caters better to the uniqueness of individuals. The winning talent strategy is to quickly assemble and reassemble the right building blocks so as to meet a business's emergent needs. Continual renewal and reinvention is the capability du jour which we explore further in Part II.

As we saw in the origins of work, our industrial-age beliefs were formed on a false understanding of human motivation. 'Adam Smith's ideas about human nature were much more invention than discovery. His argument for what people were like was false. But they gave rise to a process of industrialisation that made them true,' writes psychologist Barry Schwartz. This regretfully has shaped the nature of today's workplace and has impoverished us instead of lifting us up.

In modelling our workplace on the thesis that people are inherently lazy and spurred solely by dangling carrots, we turned a myth into a reality. We removed the soul from the organisation and replaced it with ego.

Shapers seek to perform those activities that give them the chance to learn and grow. Purposeful work is a responsibility because it betters themselves and society.

This applies across the spectrum no matter what collar you wear. Happy workers perform better. When people are more satisfied with their jobs, they are happier with their lives. There's greater commitment, increased productivity, and more profitability.

A comprehensive study of retail companies has demonstrated that the low pay, poor benefits, wacky schedules, and dignity robbing that is typical of jobs in this sector can, and more to the point should, be avoided. A *good jobs strategy* is one that makes a long-term investment in people through better pay, ongoing training, and the intrinsic motivation that comes with autonomy. This yields better financial performance for investors, morale for employees, and positive experiences for customers.

The irony is how many human resource departments fail to grasp this. It's all too common to hear of ill-fated or repeatedly delayed performance reviews, inclusion programmes parading as PR stunts, shoddy benefit packages, and the wrong people (or certainly not all the right people) leading the hiring process. The broken function of the conventional HR trade is one of the main obstacles to securing talent for well-suited positions.

CULTURE BROKERS

The function of the talent manager is not to promote a job but to sell the company DNA to the most fitting candidate. HR is really a marketing initiative; the product is the company and the consumer is the future employee. 'Good talent managers think like business-people and innovators first, and like HR people last,' insists Patty Mccord, former Chief Talent Officer at Netflix. A successful campaign results in identifying and selecting applicants who have the potential to adapt and grow.

So instead of hiring staff largely based on the boxes they check, talent managers must consider an alternative approach. They must seek out and lure candidates that are eager to create and skill up in categories yet to be defined. 'Companies want misfits, yet they want to hire them the old-fashioned way. They want revolutionaries, yet they want their most conservative leaders to identify them,' says storyteller Jeff Wasiluk.

> HR is really a marketing initiative; the product is the company and the consumer is the future employee.

Progressive talent managers should ask themselves:

➤ Can our employees galvanise around an authentic, clear, and compelling purpose?

➤ Do we positively treat our people like adults?

➤ What does our company culture say about us as a destination to work?

➤ What specific functions do we need to perform and how can we resource them in the smartest and most ethical way?

➤ Is the traditional 40-hour week the optimum way for us to utilise all or part of our workforce and, more importantly, enable them up to do their best work? Is a shorter work week or job sharing an option for us?

➤ How does a distributed workforce and remote work enable us to advance our mission and let our people do their best work?

➤ Do dynamic external workforces (talent networks) provide a viable solution to meet our current and future needs? And if so, how do we build an inclusive culture that treats these workers right?

'Employee Experience Design' is the cheeky catch-all answer. A relatively newish approach evolving over the past two decades, it is much more integrated: employer branding, interviewing, on-boarding, 360 feedback, perks and rewards, wellness, events, mentorship, training, off-boarding, and anything that will enhance the working environment and experience for an employee. The ushers of this modernised practice are no longer Chief Human

Resource Officers, nor so much even talent managers, they are *People and Culture Brokers.*

Such brokers ensure that those destined to work most closely with the new candidates are involved in the hiring process. Some even ditch the resumé in favour of really getting to know a candidate through 'try before you buy' approaches like wine and cheese parties, day-long workshops, or short work assignments. Indeed, when hiring managers have access to so much revealing data, it's increasingly challenging for anyone to fake it. Companies can gauge a candidate's potential fit, and the candidate can discern if a company is all it's cracked up to be.

Recruiters must tell a gripping story that attracts the new candidates they seek. The most effective way to do this is by inspiring existing staff so they do the bulk of the marketing. More than 30% of required skills on job specifications are rarely met, so recruiters need to be less picky about finding all the right skills in a single candidate. It's those candidates with an insatiable hunger to learn–rather than ones that just meet job descriptions–that are the true rock stars.

COMPANIES LIVING THEIR VALUES

One of the most dynamic recruitment strategies hails from the pioneering Dutch healthcare company *Buurtzorg.* All nurses within a team (of up to 12) must unanimously agree on hiring any new member. The bond between nurses is so extraordinary because they ensure all new additions are 100% committed and reliable. When it comes to providing care to patients, it's imperative they have confidence with those they work alongside. Buurtzorg's unprecedented levels of care and massive cost savings are possible in part because of the entrepreneurial creativity granted to nurses. It's also the main reason why the model of neighbourhood care is going global.

What about those times when someone is hired and it turns out to be a snafu? Online shoe retailer Zappos offers $2000 to candidates to quit after the first week of training if they decide the company isn't quite their bag. It's a smart recruiting move. The company recognises the high costs of training and if it's apparent that the candidate isn't working out, they can cut their losses early and avoid further costs. Amazon (which acquired Zappos in 2009) has since adopted the practice, dubbing it 'pay to quit'. Instead of a one-time deal during training, fulfilment centre employees get the offer each year where the payout increases by $1000 (up to a maximum of $5000).

Zappos also employs the 'Nice Guy Test'. A clever way to reveal this is from the Zappos shuttle driver. If a potential candidate is rude to the driver on the way to the interview, you can be sure that Jack or Jill ain't getting that gig.

To wrap it all together and really transmit its culture, a company must live its values. In 2014, leading pharmacy, CVS, decided to stop selling cigarettes. As a healthcare company, CEO Larry Merlo claimed the practice was inconsistent with its purpose. That kind of bold move may have resulted in billions of lost sales, but it helped shape a consistent story that employees, stakeholders, consumers, and the public can rally around. A year later, CVS was ranked number 7 on the Fortune 500 list, with revenue jumping to $153.3 billion USD.

Or take Southwest Airlines. The airline industry is often criticised for grumpy employees and poor customer service (and, yes, sometimes even dragging

> What's essential today for healthy company culture is the transparency of a true value exchange.

uncooperative passengers off the plane). A celebrated Harvard Business Review case of Southwest revealed that the airline's culture was extraordinary. While other airlines permitted their financial numbers to dictate their expansion plans before they addressed their corporate culture, Southwest built, and sustained, its spirited culture first. Regardless of the pressure to expand, the behemoth only grew if it could simultaneously uphold company values. Turns out, Southwest is inspired to go that extra mile.

In one business, gifting customers with financial rewards might get you fired. At the Ritz Carlton, well-known for giving up to $2000 per employee to spend on customer delight, it can get you promoted. A company's culture is informed by the norms, rituals, behaviours, and unwritten rules that govern any community. What's essential today for healthy company culture is the transparency of a true value exchange. The psychological contracts that weighted heavily in favour of the organisation are giving way to new ones better balanced with the employee.

GOING HOLLYWOOD

Lifetime loyalty to a single company has gone the way of the dodo bird. And progressive companies that cater to the human impulse to be free are the ones that will prosper in the future. Taking their cue from the Hollywood model, the shapers in these organisations work seamlessly with a myriad of worker types. Like a movie production, their WD-40 is flexibility.

They appreciate that to get the best out of people, they must let them design their own approach to work. It's not debatable, but a basic reality of human nature. Assuming there is the volition (desire to do good work), there must be the right conditions–fertile ground for folks to get on with making their best contribution.

When work seeps into the fabric of life, there is only so much, if anything at all, that humans will tolerate as 'managed resources'. The benefit an individual brings is their individuality. As such, they should not be wriggled to fit into the firm but celebrated for their unique gifts and stretched so as to make their greatest contributions.

The story a company tells must remain consistent with the values of its employees. And if there is misalignment, then engagement and productivity will suffer. The most talented will jump ship. But when employees can rally around a shared vision, they become the lifeblood of the organisation. When they are ennobled by great teammates and bold leaders, they become more themselves. They become shapers–acting as active agents for the company instead of empty vessels.

A film production enables individuals to make their best contribution. It provides space for them to find meaning in what they do. If more of our workplaces were modelled like this, we would be shaping our human nature in the same spirit.

Nearly half of all US workers are now millennials and by 2025, that percentage will jump to 75%. In comparison, the prior generation represented just 16% of the workforce in their time. Not only do younger workers tend to be more optimistic, their worldview has been defined in the digital era. These bourgeoning shapers are set on creating a working life where they come alive. The big difference now is that they have the opportunity and drive to do so.

CHAPTER 5

THE DRIVE TO WORK

While our ancestors saw work as a sacrifice that made them morally worthy, shapers see work as a moral good that is worthy in and of itself. They want to get better at what they do, connect with others and with their purpose, and feel free to do work that matters. As such, the key to long-term professional performance stems from having a powerful inner drive.

In the early 20th century, Robert Woodworth, a student of renowned philosopher and psychologist William James, proposed that something could be performed as a function of its own drive. This system of dynamic psychology made room for both our *behaviour* and our *consciousness* of a given activity.

Later, Abraham Maslow designed his famous hierarchy, mapping out the basic growth needs starting with those necessary for survival. For some, the self-actualising endeavour of work, with its space for creativity and problem solving, sits pretty well at the top. Yet Maslow never intended the path to personal bliss to be so quaintly staged, nor to be represented as a pyramid. Towards the end of his life he argued that self-transcendence was the apex: putting your own needs aside and serving something greater than yourself. Over a lifetime, you might shift back and forth within the hierarchy and address several needs simultaneously.

With their self-determination theory, Edward Deci and Richard Ryan built upon Maslow's work. Here, motivation rests on three innate psychological needs that shape our behaviour: 1) competence; 2) relatedness; and 3) autonomy. When these three criteria are met, one is poised to continually grow and discover meaning.

More recently, Barry Schwartz and organisational psychologist Amy Wrzesniewski found that work activities can have internal and instrumental *consequences* but this doesn't necessarily mean that those who thrive at work have internal and instrumental *motives*. In their research with cadets at the US Military Academy at West Point, they concluded that 'Cadets with strong internal and strong instrumental motives for attending West Point performed worse on every measure than did those with strong internal motives but weak instrumental ones. They were less likely to graduate, less outstanding as military officers and less committed to staying in the military.' In other words, while status and a paycheck may be the *consequences* of why you work, the real signal of your contribution and progress comes from what *motivates* you.

We actually stunt our professional progress when we allow ourselves to be led by both intrinsic and extrinsic drivers. The key to long-term professional performance is having a powerful inner drive. Medellin-based writer and shaper David Kadavy explains: 'I've decided what I want to do with my life ... to follow my curiosity and see where it takes me. To learn what I can and share that. I arrived here because I tried a lot of things—all that was left was finding pleasure in my work.' Once he found what lit him up, he doubled down on his writing life and has never looked back.

The science behind human motivation should inform how we organise ourselves in work. And although there is no one-size-fits-all solution for a company, we can think in systems with the interconnectedness of control, context, and collaboration.

1. Control

Engaged employees have more discretion over their experiences at work. We've seen the power of autonomy at work: being trusted to choose when, where, and how we work is vital for workers to feel and be their best. Still, the use of fixed technology (a desk phone and a desktop tied to a workstation) exceeds mobile technology (a cell phone and a laptop) by 2 to 1. Office desks around the world are not only restricting mobility, they're doubling as handcuffs.

2. Context

What works in Barcelona won't necessarily fly in Bengaluru. The most engaged employees in the world are in emerging economies. Developed nations are more polarised (either very engaged or not at all) and a few notables like Spain, Belgium, and France suffer from the highest rates of dissatisfaction. When a company expands to a new city, and 'exports' its office, it must consider cultural context. Too often, companies fail to appreciate the nuances of a city's culture and meet the expectations of their future employees. This principle even extends to large office settings that span several floors. When someone, say in Customer Success (2nd floor), heads up to Management (22nd floor), the cultural disparity, more than the physical distance, can be telling of organisational dysfunction.

3. Collaboration

Paradoxically, many companies still operate with stiff hierarchies that inhibit collaboration. Collective efforts that fuel the innovation economy don't jive well with the positional authority that is so commonplace. What's needed in turn is a dynamic and participatory way of working that champions cognitive and cultural diversity, multiple opinions, and a knack for adapting to change.

Organisational agility is like a pendulum, and as it swings, experimentation is required to keep people engaged. Sensitivity must be given to the emergent properties and uniqueness of each institution. Those companies that champion control, context, and collaboration lay the foundation for people to be their best selves. They convert the proverbial office into a destination where employees choose to work and hangout.

While our ancestors saw work as a sacrifice that made them morally worthy, shapers see work as a moral good that is worthy in and of itself. Whether team leader or YouTuber, the main driver for being engaged in our work comes deep from within. And as organisations upgrade their operating systems, we too must continually update our personal ones. When we sync with our motivations, we can discover more meaning, build better organisations, and weave a richer social fabric.

With some history under our belt and an appreciation for how the nature of work is changing, we turn our attention to the ways in which one's job and one's personal life have blended. It's possible to organise ourselves in such a fashion that finding and sustaining purposeful work as shapers may not be for the few but a real opportunity for the masses.

CHAPTER 6
WORK-LIFE BLEND

As work and life have blended, we need to be increasingly discerning in how we expend our energy. In the case of traditional workaholics who toil away as a diversion, engaged workaholics do so as an energiser. By working in intervals, cross-training between domains, and adopting the right attitude–shapers seek to spiral up.

'Sup buddy?' Brian saunters into the cafe with a grin. On cue, I prep my fantastical coffee shake concoction complete with peanut butter cookie, a scoop (or two) of vanilla ice-cream, a dose of chocolate syrup, and just the right amount of espresso. Oblivious to Brian's chatter, I'm dead set on making the best thing he's ever tasted. When he indulged in one of my wacky creations, which was all too frequently for one human, the twinkle in Brian's eyes grew brighter. Then I got fired.

As a teenager, this was my first proper job. A barista was the perfect position for me–I loved people and would soon grow to love coffee as well. I moved on to a myriad of other jobs: retail slave, warehouse packer, bartender, salesman, marketer, event organiser, designer, researcher, innovation guy, teacher, lecturer–you name it and I likely did, or at the very least tried it. For a hot minute I worked at a startup that was trying to take down Google. Big surprise, they went bust.

In all of these roles I was a *segmentor*: work was work and I got my kicks in life and satisfaction elsewhere. Segmentors keep the space between work and life wholly separate because having them bleed together feels unsettling.

In the fall of 2003, at the same time that the Concorde made its last supersonic flight, I started a business. I moved from a *segmentor* to a *blender*–and an entirely rubbish one at that. For the better part of a decade, I would direct all of my energy (and I had a tonnes of it) towards work. Indeed, work had become a container for my fear of failure and totally consumed me.

It took a while and a lot of practice, but I think that I'm a much better *blender* now. I strive to integrate work and life in such a fashion that the two are in harmony, often indistinguishable from one another. While the seamlessness can get tricky at times, it can also bring wholeheartedness. Diplomat, historian, and writer François-René de Chateaubriand put it best:

> A master in the art of living draws no sharp distinction between their work and their play, their labour and their leisure, their mind and their body; their education and their recreation. They hardly know which is which. They simply pursue their vision of excellence through whatever they are doing, and leave others to determine whether they are working or playing. To themselves, they always appear to be doing both.

DO THE RIGHT THING

If we are what we repeatedly do, then the question *blenders* ask is: 'How can I best direct my energy today?' The answer, it seems, isn't about doing things the right way–it's about doing the right thing.

The workplace has become an abstract concept with a virtual set of relations. The office now lives in our pockets or purses. And what you do, rather than where you go, is what really matters. Eking out your waking hours so as to get the best results is what keeps you relevant.

Shapers are in effect masterful *blenders*. Instead of working around the clock, *blenders* layer work into life like expert Tetris players. With a war chest of resilience, they continually level up.

At the risk of sounding drunk on my own Kool-Aid, I should clarify that *the blend* is about a distinct working style that blurs work and life in a purposeful way. It means moving fluidly between facets of work and life aligning your skills, interests, hobbies, and attitudes in such a fashion that you feel richer for it. Interestingly enough, the organisations that actively seek to blend work and personal time for their employees are actually better off in the long run.

Nearly half of the US professional workforce are independent workers. And we're now witnessing passionate job quitters and an entire gamut of flexible working arrangements help shape the *Great Migration*. With a tsunami of workers striking out on their own, there'll be more Tetris players than ever before.

While some take to *the blend* like a duck to water, it suits a certain skin better than others. And regardless of whether you fancy your-self a *segmentor*, *blender*, or a bit of both, what's important is that you set healthy boundaries for those things that matter most.

The new workforce is a young one. The advantage of being born after 1980 is being *native to digital* and only knowing our connected world (perhaps a drawback is never having possessed a pre-internet brain). But millennials are too often confused with being entitled rather than networked. The opportunities afforded by the information and telecommunications revolution have given these future shapers a fresh worldview: working hard doesn't necessarily mean getting ahead, ergo, I might as well do what I love.

ENGAGED WORKAHOLISM

Stroll into any hipster coffee shop on the weekend, in any city, and barring a no Wi-Fi policy you'll see heaps of conscientious folks on their laptops. Some may be students pretending to study, while others scrutinise cat videos—but I promise you, heaps of peeps are actually working. I'm one of them right now. 'Poor souls' some mutter under their breath; we can't enjoy our weekend and are forced to toil away on our devices. But poor souls, like rich pricks, are relative.

A tough day at the office was once counterbalanced with celebrating (often called drinking) or forgetting (dubbed television). Weekends were 100% sacred time to do anything but work. Shapers often choose to work weekends professing they do their best work while the rest of the working world, well, rests. They take a wholly unique attitude and approach, because work and play are often indistinguishable.

Still sceptical and think *the blend* is simply masquerading as workaholism? To shed some light on the matter it's helpful to distinguish between a workaholic (an avoidant behaviour) and an engaged workaholic (a deliberate behaviour). At the age of 28, Adam Grant became the youngest full professor at Wharton, having written over 60 peer reviewed publications and a best-selling book. His colleague Nancy Rothbard says Grant's love affair with work isn't a bad thing and doesn't guarantee burnout. An expert on the boundaries between work and life, Rothbard explains that when we find meaning in our work–seeing it as a joyous endeavour–we don't necessarily need to recover like 'unhappy workaholics'. Workaholics, the disenchanted kind, are obsessed with their jobs but don't actually like them. Work functions as a diversion.

For many, busyness has become a proxy for productivity rein-forced by the always-on diet. At time of writing, a 31-year-old Tokyo based journalist clocked 159 hours of overtime in a month. Soon thereafter she died of a heart failure. Japanese authorities declared it death by *karoshi*. The *karoshi* phenomenon was commonplace in that country's bubble economy in the 1980s and has since, rather regretfully, normalised death by overwork-ing. Western doctors call it *civilisation's disease*–a nod to the toxic ways some lead their lives.

This trend epitomises what German philosopher Joseph Pieper called *total work*–when humans become workers and nothing else. Our careers become the centre of our lives, and the totality of work takes up not just all of our time but also all of the real estate in our brains.

To be sure, there is a big difference between a shaper and a hustler. Working around the clock and wearing an 'always-on' badge with pride is the mark of a hustler. There's no time to 'turn off' when you're so 'turned on' the hustler claims. The anxiety surrounding failure is so pronounced, the default mode is simply to work harder. It's a slippery slope from finding yourself in work to having work consume you. The saner strategy of the shaper is to intentionally funnel the working spirit–toiling in bursts followed by rest and reflection.

NETWORK OF ENTERPRISES

Just as work and life are blending, so too are disciplines and industries. Is Google a search engine, advertising company or artificial intelligence company? Is Facebook a social network or political lobbyist? To be frank I don't actually know, and I'm not entirely sure it matters. What I do know is that the ability to move between and match up disciplines will be a need-to-have quality for shapers. Instead of relying on arbitrary job titles, a diverse intersection of talents will be assembled for a given project. We'll need to slip seamlessly among creative, experimental, risky, emotive, collaborative, analytical, and networked mindsets and functions.

In a study of operatic composers, psychologist Dean Keith Simonton found that the most successful composers blend genres. Instead of focusing on a particular genre of opera, the most successful composers cross-train, pulling from a rich mix of genres. Certainly, a deep expertise is always a good foundation, but we can be wary of getting too engrained in a particular field. We must widen our vision to ensure our peripheral gaze is popping.

In another instance, excessive schooling impaired creativity in writers who received a lot of formal education. At some stage they just had to make the jump and get on with it. Getting fit for a creative pursuit may best be achieved by shifting between broad interests and disparate fields. The real trick is knowing when and how to move fluidly between them.

Innovation expert Frans Johansson explains that it's a diversity of perspectives that truly drives innovation. So a helpful practice for shapers is to operate on the threshold—in between disciplines. It's in the *antidisciplinary* space, where a certain field is yet to exist, that the magic happens. Say, for example, where sociology and psychology marry—and voila! You have social psychology.

With more colourful thinking, we're more open to what psychologist Howard Gruber calls a 'network of enterprises'. Instead of a narrow focus on one question or domain, we cross-train to stay malleable. No joke: my orthodontist was also an extraordinary jeweller.

Like Simone de Beauvoir or Leonardo da Vinci, we obsess about lots of things and might pursue a series of loosely connected ideas, questions, and projects at the same time. Too much expertise can actually be detrimental to creative greatness. We've all heard the expression of not seeing the forest for the trees.

The reality of your place in work (and work's fit into your life for that matter) is ultimately determined by *how you choose to see it*. With the vantage of time, you can see yourself persisting (and perhaps prospering) into the future.

Holocaust survivor and psychiatrist Viktor Frankl knew all too well that the only things keeping him (and his fellow prisoners in the concentration camps) alive was the yearning to be reunited with loved ones and/or the opportunity to put creative works into the world. Our thoughts shape our reality and no matter what the circumstances, we can adopt whatever attitude we choose.

We turn our attention now to the modalities of work that are more becoming to the shaper life and the wired world we live in. At the frontier of the future of the work movement, we'll consider why dynamic teams and adaptive organisations do what they do so well. And we'll start to reveal that it's how we organise and work that requires constant experimentation. The overarching aim is for us to serve up the absolute best taco we got.

PART II

BETTER WAYS OF WORKING

The only way to make sense out of change is to plunge into it, move with it and join the dance.

—Alan Watts

Better ways of working are dependent on trust. Since the prover-bial office is now more a state of mind, we explore the desire, discipline and determination needed to do our best work. Shapers appreciate how to continually craft a career, pursue dopeness, work fluidly, manage themselves and employ the right tools with the right temperament at the right time. The end game is to ride high and set the stage for doing the work that matters most.

CHAPTER 7

BAD BOSSES

The biggest destroyer of meaningfulness at work is bad bosses. Different styles of leadership premised on either hoarding control or giving it away can mean the difference between a deflated or motivated employee. The most dynamic leaders not only know this, they live it every day.

Glenn Elliott likes sporting a t-shirt which reads 'Bad bosses ruin lives'. After a decade in corporate life, he fled to set up a company to do something about the rampant disengagement he witnessed. When it comes to killing motivation at work, he knows all too well that the guilty culprit is often that manager from hell.

Research from MIT demonstrated that while the quality of leadership is rarely mentioned when people talk about meaningful moments at work, bad management is the 'top destroyer of meaningfulness'. Good leaders can often go unnoticed, but it's hard to ignore the bad ones who suck the sense of purpose from their staff.

Think of the charismatic salesman who gets promoted to Regional Sales Manager (as often is the case in companies with high performers). He's not experienced nor equipped to be an effective manager. His past clients may notice a decline in service, but more to the point, his new reports must tolerate the consequences of his dreadful management style. This same old story is replicated in countless organisations. The potential damage of this kind of hyper-critical leadership goes well beyond unmotivated employees. It contributes to serious physical issues including depression, high blood pressure, weight gain, substance abuse, and even premature death.

The real shocker is that most of those captains at the helm of the company ship don't have what it takes to be a 21st century leader. The so-called *Peter Principle* can help explain why: 'managers tend to rise up in the organisation to the stage of their respective incompetence'. Once thought to be a light-hearted theory at best, new evidence proves this principle to be very real.

In stark contrast, effective managers let their workers decide how to direct their energy so as to best advance the company's vision. They are the special kind of manager that can fastidiously adapt to change and reorganise to better serve their teams. They are more empathetic and charismatic and able to motivate and support others to perform at their best. This breed of leader, as we'll see in Chapter 16, seeks to enrich the working spirit rather than quash it.

Flocks of workers flee spirit sapping offices since they 'Dislike having bosses: the prospect of not having one, surveys have shown, is a major motivation for going freelance. Having the freedom to work where you want, in your own time, rather than among people and in a place not of your choosing, are things that people increasingly value, and not only those at the top end of the pay-scale,' writes William Skidelsky in the *Financial Times*.

Trusting workers, and giving them more discretion over their work, is not just a dainty ethical practice–it's an economic strategy too. Beth Comstock, a shaper and former Vice Chair of General

Electric, knows this. She developed *The Culture Club* (no, not a fan group for the new wave band). It's a multilevel group in her business unit to help with transformational change and leadership. She gives teams a 'bounty' to bring her something that she really doesn't want to hear about. With this level of candour, leaders can identify which inefficiencies can be eliminated or reduced. And by creating this safe space for everyone to give constructive feedback without the fear of being pooh-poohed, teams can grow, worker well-being is elevated, and business innovation is unlocked.

Y MARKS THE SPOT

Social psychologist Douglas McGregor categorises leaders into two distinct types. Theory X managers are distrustful and typically micromanage. These are authoritarian types, ruling from fear and with an iron fist. They believe people dislike work and have little ambition.

Theory Y managers believe that people have the agency, desire, capacity, creativity, and resourcefulness to do great work. They instil high levels of confidence in their teams, are inclusive, and employ a participatory management style. When they feel the fear, they rise to the challenge with courage.

In most companies, Theory X and Y style management coexists. For starters, different managers may employ both styles and switch between the two depending on the situation. But the overall culture of an organisation tends to one style or another.

Under the leadership of Sundar Pichai, Google practises Y management–giving control to workers to do their work and be their best. At the same time, the company is renowned for making some employees feel like they operate within a golden age. It's just not so black and white as what management style a company, or a given manager for that matter, may pursue.

Super selective micromanagers are those who might give incredible leeway in one instance or be overly controlling in another. Amazon's Jeff Bezos epitomises this duality, ruling firmly but strategically by blending both styles. Just like their products, he's constantly tweaking and optimising his people. His Y-style leadership gives runway to workers such that they can turn something like the flop that was the Amazon phone into the astonishing achievement that is Alexa.

In the same breath, many Amazon employees report being tethered to a pager, while those who work in warehouses complain of having to move with the agility of linebackers instead of pickers and packers. Bezos' tactics might be a great strategy to innovate and scale, but they are not necessarily compatible with growing most people. We humans are quirky and don't run on data points.

More and more we are seeing how workers are motivated by the results they might achieve as well as intrinsic benefits. Subsequently, Theory Y-oriented managers seek to sync the goals of the individual with those of the organisation. They understand that when folks feel a genuine sense of belonging, when they have space to learn what they need to know to do their best work, they bring their A-game.

Hard-ass Theory X managers can try to be trusting on demand, but in the long run, that won't fly. Shapers intuitively know when their boss is standing in the way of doing great work and to be sure something will need to give.

Trust isn't doled out when it's most convenient, it's a two-way street of respect that must be mutually earned. Theory X leaders who act as if people will only perform when ruled by a carrot and stick will soon discover that employees won't stick around.

When pinned against horrible bosses, shapers must get seriously creative. This may mean an extraordinary rejigging of work. As we will now see, this is job crafting with finesse. Holding a point of view where you believe you have, or will have, the ability to make a contribution is so important. Sometimes leaving is the answer and other times, just as for many relationships, you may be exporting the same old problems to a new scenario.

CHAPTER 8

THE PURSUIT OF DOPENESS

We can achieve dopeness through small gains and a commitment to continuously learn, practise, and improve. Should you hold a job you don't particularly like, with some ingenuity it may be possible to turn it into one you come to love. As their badass selves, shapers are willing to actively engage with the unknown time and time again.

He was the mastermind that helped sell 72,000 units of Beyonce's Heat perfume in an hour. This was back in 2010 and the man behind the scenes working his magic was shaper Marcus Collins. Today, he is an executive at a Motor City (Detroit, Michigan) advertising firm and a marketing professor at the University of Michigan's Ross School of Business where he teaches a new generation about social engagement.

Collins is a better academic because he's a practitioner and vice versa. The thread that ties his careers together is in an unrelenting curiosity and desire to understand people. 'All I want is dopeness,' is what Collins says when I ask about his unrelenting drive. Whether gracing the stage at conferences, scooping up advertising awards, supporting students, raising his kid, completing his doctorate, or helping out his church, pursuing dopeness is the guiding principle for his life.

Achieving 'dopeness' is really an age-old idea dating back to Aristotle's *eudaimonia*. Loosely translating to human flourishing, *eudaimon* is all about living in good spirits. It can extend to your higher self by achieving your unique potential. And it also entails persevering in the face of adversity. Likewise, dopeness can be realised through small gains and the commitment to continuously learn, practise, and improve. There may be countless posts touting how to hack your way there, but the real question lies in whether you'll show up and do the work. For shapers, the answer is an unequivocal yes—the key to living well turns when its virtuously earned.

If we're really serious about pursuing excellence, we need to put an end to the God-awful habit of multitasking. It's proven to make us less efficient. We fool ourselves into believing we're doing many things simultaneously when in reality we're just switching between tasks super-fast. We're fracturing our attention because we're still thinking of the previous task when we embark on the new one. 'Studies using fMRI technology to view brain activity have found that it's impossible to do two things at once, even in individuals who claim to be exceptional multitaskers. What's really happening is that your brain is either dividing and conquering, dedicating only half of its available horsepower to each task, or constantly switching between tasks. Either way, your output level suffers, as does the quality of your work,' writes performance expert Brad Stulberg. This is precisely why we do well to work in intervals, just as athletes train.

A QUALITY ONLY YOU CONTROL

OK, so maybe like me, from time to time you wander off daydreaming of being a food critic or nature photographer. Whatever your fantasy, I'm sure you indulge once in a while. That's OK. The point is this: your view of yourself in work will always be biased. We're all influenced by social cues, professional standards, a tireless media–and perhaps most of all, our inner critics. I might not actually get paid to taste ice cream, but I did take my friends to a Sicilian Gelateria for the finest ice cream of our lives.

The opportunities to indulge our curiosity in work have never been greater. In the end, how we feel about our work is up to us and if we don't like the story we're telling ourselves it may be time to flip the script. There are so many ways to integrate our hopes and dreams into our working lives. The trick is to rock steady with doing the work that matters while staying open to new possibilities and searching for better ways to show up in the world. The dopeness will emerge. Pressing Collins on his vision for the future of work, he replied, 'A classroom where we're always growing to be better.'

Bad managers can be a real drag. So can disenchanted colleagues that relish moaning about work. But if we really want to ease the disengagement crisis, we'll need to start with ourselves. With over 175 cognitive biases at play, your own story of your place in the world is inherently skewed by how you choose to see things. Yet what never waivers is this: when you're cognisant that your work matters and happily engaged in what you do, you perform better. Ultimately, you decide how you feel about your work. The possibilities of work, the sorrows and joys, are psychological.

When you're truly engaged in your work, instead of saying 'I have to go to work', you say 'I get to go to work'. Your family, friends, and colleagues all take notice. When you are hardwired to operate from this genuine place of purpose, it has a glowing butterfly effect. That inner smirk manifests as an outer beam. Envious onlookers want some of what you're having.

When it comes down to motivation the trick is to find ways to continually inspire yourself. Muses can help. Whichever way you renew yourself, it's about taking a step back to reveal whether you truly have autonomy in your work, find it meaningful, continue to learn, and dig who you work with. All of these play integral roles in propelling you to be your best.

MANAGING TASKS
WHEN YOU HAVE
AUTONOMY

MANAGING TASKS
WHEN YOU DON'T
HAVE AUTONOMY

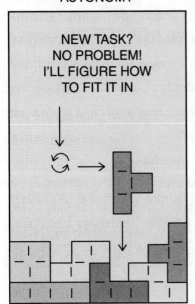

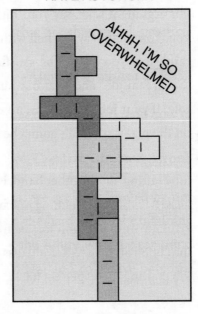

Fosslien, L. and West Duffy, M. (2019) *No Hard Feelings*. New York: Portfolio/Penguin. Also see https://www.instagram.com/lizandmollie

Reinventing work so that disenchanted employees become fully engaged won't happen overnight. It'll likely happen only for some, over time, and probably through small wins. While we've seen that why we work is for both intrinsic and instrumental rewards, it's internal motivations that can have the greatest impact on performance. Without the agency to control our work, the feelings of progress will remain illusory.

For some, disengagement will be best solved by changing jobs. For argument sake, say your highly disturbed boss enjoys baiting you. You might say the hell with it, pick up, and quit. Or you may think that you should be satisfied because society says you have the 'dream job' and beat out hundreds of others for this coveted role. If your job truly sucks, no matter how much lipstick you put on the pig–it still ain't gonna be pretty.

Job crafting, on the other hand, is another route to achieving dopeness. It involves something much more subtle yet remarkably powerful: turning that god forsaken job you have (nasty boss and all) into one you love. After all, dissatisfaction breeds innovation and job crafting is the perfect hack.

The concept, developed by psychologists Amy Wrzesniewski and Jane E. Dutton, involves taking the components of your job and redesigning them to better align with your talent and interests through a three-tiered framework:

1. **Task crafting:** *changing your activities and day-to-day tasks.*
2. **Relational crafting:** *remodelling your relationship with others to change your perspective on why you do a particular job.*
3. **Cognitive crafting:** *reframing how you see work and the interactions you have with others to open up new opportunities.*

Job crafting has led many people to find more meaning in their work. In one extraordinary case, a hospital cleaner took it upon herself to perform many activities in addition to her usual duties. She would regularly dust the ceilings so patients didn't have to stare at the dirt or cobwebs. She would often take water to thirsty patients between nursing shift changes. For comatose patients, she would even change their surroundings in the hopes that it might improve their well-being (or potentially help wake them up). This cleaner saw herself not just as a cleaner but as a caretaker. Expanding her job, within reason, enabled her to derive much more dopeness.

Employees, managers, customers, and the company as a whole can reap the benefits of job crafting. Indeed, it's fast becoming a necessity because:

> ➤ *Being fulfilled at work translavtes into an engaged workforce, which correlates with productivity.*
>
> ➤ *The quality of jobs over the quantity is what matters in the long haul for companies and the world.*
>
> ➤ *When the values of the individual align with their work, meaning can ensue, providing variety, autonomy, challenge, feedback on performance, and the opportunity to see and feel progress.*

There are plenty of obstacles to becoming a successful job crafter. Business conditions may be just too toxic to permit fruitful job crafting. But for those progressive organisations that continue to hire for *hunger* over *talent* while granting more discretion to employees within their work, job crafting will prove to be invaluable. After all, a business cannot innovate if everyone within it remains static.

GUMBY TIME

In the early 1980s, management oracle Charles Handy predicated that work would become more bitty and fractured. His portfolio worker–a lifestyle choice that is now the norm–has led to an endless array of personalised life paths. While it may be a luxury to make a living as an organic Kombucha brewer serving hot yoga patrons, there is no shame in contemplating meaning in work.

When having five different careers in a lifetime is now standard, and even advised by the *Financial Times*, the road once less travelled is now bumper to bumper. Persistent job crafters are in effect system designers, seeking to mix and remix the pieces of an endless work puzzle. They retrofit their work so as to make it more compatible with their unique passions, strengths, and values. Indeed, many are fast becoming like Gumby, stretching and re-shaping their careers in real-time.

Sometimes the biggest catalyst for dopeness comes from constraints. Whether it's a hard deadline or family obligations, pressures (either set by yourself or others) help you to be more inventive and, rather ironically, open up new possibilities.

With the continued rise of the global independent workforce, career shaping will be necessary to fuel oneself. The challenge becomes knowing precisely how. Whether inside or outside the company, shaping a meaningful working life is a evolutionary practice. It's through this struggle that the rewards come. And the degree to which you shape your work and expand yourself is something only you control.

CHAPTER 9
VITAL INGREDIENTS

We're changing jobs more frequently than ever before and pursuing multiple careers and projects simultaneously. While a solid skillset is a great place to start, it's a knack for adapting that differentiates shapers from the crowd. To thrive at work we need to become fluid–moving quickly with dexterity amid constant change. It's this trait more than anything else that makes shapers indispensable.

Martin Short is one of the few people in comedy who's also capable of laughing on both the outside and the inside. Born near Toronto, Short is the youngest of five children. When he was 12 years old, his eldest brother died in a car accident. Six years later, his mother died of cancer, and two years after that his father passed away from a stroke. His wife of 30 years died of cancer at age 58. Despite all this, Short still demonstrates an unparalleled *joie de vivre*–he just keeps moving forward. 'No one is any one thing,' sums up his outlook on life.

During appearances on popular shows like 'The Tonight Show Starring Jimmy Fallon' and 'Jimmy Kimmel Live!' he invariably has his host in stitches. Ever the comic's comic, Short's brand of in-the-moment zaniness doesn't happen without a set of tools. And his toolbox is mighty big.

Whether performing a duet with Steve Martin, embarrassing Drake, or playing a host of oddball characters, he is always experimenting and learning. Tom Hanks tells the story of the first time he saw Short. The comic was standing on a chair working a room full of professional funny people. It was some bigwig's soiree and absolutely everyone was in hysterics. That is because Short welcomes change and continually takes risks. He knows how to engineer serendipity. The comedic chameleon may well be the funniest man alive.

It's this same strain of continuous reinvention that helps shapers thrive. Work is now a process and practice to improve. You must demonstrate the fortitude that comes with owning a growth mindset so that you can stay indispensable. Short teaches us that we must play and create–because it makes us stronger. It makes us more human.

MODERN MODALITIES

A marked departure from the rigid ways of the past, the new mode of work is much more fluid. It allows us to handle more ambiguity and complexity. With the modern ways of working we consistently tap into our cognitive powers, creative energy, and collective genius so we can soar. It's this fluidity, a learned practice that ebbs and flows, which is the hallmark modality of the new world of work.

> **Fluidity:** the ability to move quickly and with dexterity amid constant change.

Being fluid is a sign of strength in times of uncertainty. We move like water; flowing in harmony with everything we encounter. Those that shine in the workplace move with similar ease. Cultivating fluidity means seeking change, continuously improving, all the while expertly navigating towards a future that's only coming at us faster.

In many ways, fluidity is just a mental construct rooted in Darwinian logic. Learning to adapt and change with grace helps us stay equanimous when everything is in constant flux. We are courageous, speedy, and effective. Indeed, others are drawn to shapers because they find our self-assurance and spirit intoxicating.

The resurgence of stoicism also signals a desire to live more fluidly. We're yearning to lead deeper and richer lives. Looking through a stoic lens helps us write and rewrite those stories that let us navigate uncertainty with more ease. The challenge, of course, is that this is all easier said than done. Roman philosopher Seneca would surely be rolling his eyes at many of us: 'Suffer more often in the imagination than in reality.'

Like Martin Short, taking a diverse and nimble approach to work is one way to deal with volatility. 'If our economy is to be innovative, creative and diverse in thought, then so too must our education, our workforce and our jobs. If we are to have breakthrough technologies, we need to create breakthrough thinkers with the capacity to understand a variety of fields,' writes researcher Joshua Krook. Having a solid skillset is a good start, but it's really the ability to learn new skills on the go that differentiates you from the crowd. The capability of mastering and moving fluidly between different disciplines will be a hallmark of tomorrow's shapers.

VITAL INGREDIENTS

Companies like design firm IDEO and *The Economist* magazine have 30% of their workforces made up of independent workers. And perhaps the most adept, Google boasts more contractors than full-timers, with an average employee tenure of just 1.1 years. People function like Apps on a smartphone, sitting pretty on top of the company's operating system (OS). They are selected, downloaded, updated, shared, and deleted on demand.

These apps may be curated, cut, chopped, stirred, added, mixed, stewed, reconfigured, removed, folded, simmered, and toasted on demand. The robustness of this OS and the fluidity of the Apps has become an intricate dance to crack.

Like Apps, the onus falls on us to safeguard our positioning. We want to ensure we're featured on the *homescreen* all the while protecting our freedoms. 'While the production line worker lived in a world of small units in which each movement and each unit of time repeated itself until clocking off time–or even until retirement time–the world of the flexible worker is dynamic and malleable. [O]ur lives tend to break down into individual episodes. Whether these can all be stitched together into a coherent story is up to us. Or if we fail, it's up to our therapists, who we give the task of moulding wholesome unity out of the fragments,' writes Sebastian Pranz.

Companies continue to shimmy and shuffle to attract talent, while we continue to search for meaning and challenge. We can insulate ourselves against existential dread. These are the vital INGREDI-ENTS to help shapers remain featured on the home screen:

Intuiting: Sometimes working things out by intuition and learning to trust our gut.

Noting: Bear witness, observe, pause, respond, refuse, and choose from a place of wisdom. Practise self-awareness so that we can direct our focus to those things that makes our minds soar and our hearts sing. Remain cognisant of our teammates and the entire organisation.

Giving: Commit to something greater than ourselves. Dedication can't be faked and companies can smell it from miles away. Let the care we have and the quality of our work do the talking.

Relating: Connect with others for depth not breadth. Building meaning-ful relationships is enlightened self-interest at work. It helps us build a safety net that provides the confidence to create our personal flywheel for doing our best and deepest work.

Expanding: See the world with wide eyes and remain open to possibili-ties, understand situations from another's point of view, and let go of our egos to curiously engage with the unknown.

Discerning: Time is finite. The trick is to be ruthless in managing our energy, so that it can expand and become boundless.

Integrating: Give life to a myriad of projects that we are valued for and that fuel our inner working lives. Combine and recombine as needed.

Expressing: Be a good steward to our unique gifts. Create, experiment, and serve ourselves and others with gumption.

Navigating: The tenacity to engage with the unknown and constantly stretch our capabilities through training, novel experiences, high contrast conversations, experimentation, and feedback. Showing courage to step out of our comfort zones and never rest on our laurels.

Trusting: Nothing fruitful in the long term comes without integrity. Trust is earned with courage, over time, and by reputation. There is no quick hack.

Sensing: At the individual, collective and global level appreciating what's needed in any given moment–and then having the audacity to show up wholeheartedly.

The grand intention here is to become unflappable. Compared to a typical business competency lasting 30 years in 1984, today it's more akin to five years. We're changing jobs more than ever and pursuing multiple careers and projects simultaneously. Take a moment to consider how many jobs you've had and how many careers you're yet to embark upon? Yeah–the ability to adapt and thrive at work, also known as your adaptability quotient, demands continuous learning and cultivation.

This paradigm shift in work is first and foremost a mental one. As human beings what we crave are open, fluid, and personalised systems. And the world of work is gradually opening to provide just that. What we need to be doing as shapers is listening, learning, and levelling up.

We can take a cue from Martin Short and seek equanimity. We can reset–fuel our minds, nourish our souls, and shape a new system of work. Underpinned by fluidity, it's this worldview that makes for a deeper inner life and a more becoming approach to the future of work. What we'll explore now is how being adaptive ourselves also makes for great teamwork.

CHAPTER 10
FLUID TEAMS WORK

How do we effectively share information, make wise decisions, safely experiment, and continuously learn? Through fluid teaming. Whether in a sports club, jazz band, or working group, the most effective teams have crystal clear goals, well-defined tasks, and the right skills and experience all when and where needed.

A series of quick celebratory dances by top players is what makes the National Basketball League tick. Star players often sign a two-year deal thinking they'll come in–strut their stuff–grab a ring, and be on their merry way. Off to the next club to rinse and repeat.

This way of operating places a premium on performance. Celebrated sports teams can stay consistent winners even with high personnel turnover because, 'They have been able to combine a realistic view of the often-temporary nature of the employment relationship with a focus on shared goals and long-term personal relationships–teams win when their individual members trust each other enough to prioritize team success over individual glory,' writes LinkedIn founder Reid Hoffman alongside authors Ben Casnocha and Chris Yeh. Likewise, top performers in the workplace who bring their A-game are clear from the get-go on their inputs and anticipated outputs. It's why one of Hoffman's better-known interview questions is, 'What are your plans after LinkedIn?'

The big challenge for companies seeking to move to sports team-styled ways of working is really about letting go of the permanence of a team. We tend to think about teams as *homes* and as such enmesh ourselves with our teammates. Our sense of self becomes tied to the group. The magic in designing high performing teams, however, rests in flexing their dynamism. In a fast-moving world, it's a challenge to attract the right people–and even more difficult to then let them go when their time is up.

In her book *Teaming,* Harvard professor Amy Edmondson explains that an organisation really thrives (or fails to thrive) depending on how its teams perform. Effective teams need clear goals, well-defined tasks, the right skills and experience at hand, sufficient resources, and access to support. But they also need to be *fluid.*

Fluid teamwork is on the rise in many industries. Edmondson explains that this is, 'Because the work–be it patient care, product development, customized software, or strategic decision-making–increasingly presents complicated interdependencies that have to be managed on the fly.' Due to the short-lived nature of teams today, the talent market looks a lot more like the world of professional sports.

Companies typically deliver value to their customers in small teams because they can adapt faster this way. Effective *teaming,* then, is really the knack for collaborating in fluid groupings. It's an emergent strategy and an essential competitive edge for shapers to be able to *learn* and *execute* on the go.

PLAYING IN THE BAND

When a fellow band member would jump out of key–as would occur from time to time–jazz musician Miles Davis would buck the norm. He'd play off it, forming something entirely progressive from what might otherwise be considered a blunder. In a brilliant interplay between musicians, the individual character and contributions of each member would gel in one cohesive band.

Jazz band or sports team, the message is clear: trust, diversity, and a common purpose are key elements for strong performance. Collaboration expert Alison Coward stresses how great teamwork starts with the individual and truly understanding, as well as catering to, how they work best. So it's not only talent, it's also great communication that can help teams become elite.

The more fluid the organising principles of our teams, the better they can gather, process, and act upon information. Gobbling up the rich data sets teams provide, the organisation has valuable business intelligence from which to continuously anchor decisions. Information flows where it needs to go and the company is able to generate much more value. As such, regular companies transform into stealth learning organisations.

Companies like Procter and Gamble caught on long ago. Since 2001, they have been innovating with people and teams outside of their company. They understand that the smartest folks probably don't work for them and the best research and development strategy is tapping into anyone who's willing to contribute. Through an open collaboration platform, *Connect + Develop*, they continuously enable and accelerate innovation.

Likewise, one of the reasons for Netflix's unparalleled success is their crowdsourced Netflix Prize. Started in 2006, the goal was to find a better algorithm to help predict which movie you might enjoy (in case you're curious, the first winner was a team led by AT&T engineers called 'Belkor's Pragmatic Chaos'). Today the Netflix recommendation engine is so powerful it feels like it knows you better than you know yourself.

Harnessing the wisdom of the crowd can be an extremely powerful innovation strategy. From something as trivial as Walker's Snack Food company crowdsourcing new chip flavours (Crispy Duck and Hoisin flavour anyone?) through to something as serious as Bill and Melinda Gates Foundation's Global Grand Challenge to create a toilet of the future, great ideas can come from anywhere. The only question is whether you're open and crafty enough, like Miles Davis, to decidedly integrate them.

BEING HUMAN AT WORK

A half-century ago or so, companies would look to build team camaraderie through informal social activities. Executives might meet one another's families at Christmas parties or over a round of golf. A long slog, these activities could prove beneficial when teams were more permanent. But a practice like this today would likely result in more resentment than rapport. When you're part of a team for a few weeks, a short exercise on building psychological safety may be a better use of time than a holiday party or a round of golf.

'More and more people in nearly every industry are now working on multiple teams that vary in duration, have a constantly shifting membership, and pursue moving targets,' explains Edmondson.

The Dutch healthcare provider Buurtzorg we encountered in Chapter 4 employs 10,000 nurses. The non-profit uses geographic-based team structures. In teams of 10 nurses, each unit serves about 50 patients in a small, well-defined neighbourhood. Amazingly, there are only 45 staff in the head office. Buurtzorg's community-based practice empowers teams by letting them manage themselves. Front-line nurses have both the opportunity and authority to learn and make decisions that affect their own work. The fragmented and inefficient ways of nursing give way to agility. Humanity wins over bureaucracy.

The impact of this way of working has been monumental. Buurt-zorg uses under 40% of the hours that Dutch doctors have stipulated for patient care, reduces all emergency hospital visits by

30%, and saves the Dutch healthcare system hundreds of millions of euros every year. Patients recover faster, remain in care for half the time, and become more autonomous. Buurtzorg is consistently rated employer of the year and is now the blueprint for healthcare providers the world over.

Teams that employ fluid practices can accomplish astonishing things. Military outfits might speedily take lives, while surgical teams swiftly save them. In the business world, effective *teaming* helped Airbnb enter the Cuban market in just 10 weeks. To the average onlooker it may appear that high performing teams dissolve almost as soon as they've formed. What won't be as apparent is the special sauce such teams generate to tackle the problem at hand; they take on a never-ending search for better ways to get work done.

Another clever way to work more fluidly is to bring customers in as part of your team. With well over 10,000 employees, ZARA breaks all the rules of fashion. When a shopper rejects an item, sales staff take notes and draw diagrams on ways the product could be improved. Over time, and with the advantage of thousands of stores, notable trends emerge. This continuous feedback mechanism coupled with dynamic factory operations, enables them to tweak shapes, styles, and trends in real time. To accommodate these impromptu customer needs, ZARA factories reserve up to 85% of their capacity to deal with in-season demands. Amazingly, what takes competitors nine months, ZARA achieves in just three weeks.

Challenging the status quo is part of the deal when a company signs up to build an immune system for an uncertain future. Many legacy companies still focus on cost cutting measures like 'restructuring' when they need to be investing in 'responsiveness'. ZARA's agility (and yes, the fact that they also own most of their stores) is why they sit pretty as the world's largest fashion retailer.

In *The Good Jobs Strategy*, operations professor Zeynop Ton explains that ZARA was inspired by the family-owned Spanish supermarket chain Mercadona. The shop employees dub their customers 'bosses'. Taking on the worldview of customers, they continually improve their processes, products, and experiences. What's needed for organisations and the people who power them is learning to disrupt themselves before someone else does it for them.

How to row the boat and innovate amidst uncertainty:

Operational Dexterity–designing operations for individuals, teams, and the organisation that are optimised for speed and flexibility.

A Human-Centred Approach–know-how to engage employees first so they can connect with customers in meaningful and imaginative ways.

Relentless Ingenuity–raw and applied creativity where taking risks is encouraged and failure is destigmatised.

The problems that businesses will need to solve in the future will only grow more challenging. And when talent is on the move, they can't afford to stand still to cope with more complexity; fluid teams like those of Buurtzorg or ZARA will instead become the norm. Reshaping how we work means abandoning the need to find answers and instead taking more time to ask better questions. When everyone is a leader, the business culture is one of constantly searching for better ways to do things.

The most significant shift in companies that cultivate fluid teams is how they let go of a machine-age mentality and celebrate the human spirit in its place. It's an active practice that requires identifying the right people to work with, effectively communicating, working well as individuals and as a unit, and focusing on the right things at the right time to make continuous progress.

'Beautiful organisations keep asking questions, they remain incomplete,' author Tim Leberecht aptly puts it. They are always flexing their unfair advantage through their seamless ability to share, decide, experiment, and learn. To truly unlock the potential of this new way of working, shapers know to release the participatory power that drives the self-management movement.

CHAPTER 11
MANAGING
SELF-MANAGEMENT

A bossless company sounds great in theory but is a lot harder to put in place. You achieve influence in these highly adaptive organisations not by what position you hold, but through your ability to grow. Not everyone has the thick skin sometimes required to thrive in these emotionally charged environments. But the benefits are enticing: more engagement, better collaboration, increased productivity, and happier workers.

In an episode from the British television series 'Black Mirror', Lacie has her every interaction rated on a five-star scale. Her friends rate her likeability, the barista rates her banter, and a job interviewer rates her employability. Through augmented reality and an ever-present social media platform, her societal worth is laid bare for all to see. Depending on her score, she gains perks and access to certain social functions, services, and opportunities. The episode is called 'Nosedive' and if you haven't seen it, the title might give you a sense on how things go.

This may be a spooky dystopian future but it's not too far-fetched. Already, we live in a reputation economy: influence is achieved by demonstrating just how good you are. Your perceived influence determines if you get a loan or car, if you'll get hired and with what pay, and may even affect your marriage prospects. Who listens to you, how you're viewed, where you can go, and what you can get–are in many ways–influence by your 'score.'

While the 'Black Mirror' episode forces us to reckon with the serious consequences of the reputation economy, it does present us with some interesting possibilities in the workplace–namely the ability to break down hierarchies and allow employees to manage their own workflows. Useless posturing doesn't overshadow productivity. Here, there are fewer scorecards of who did which favour for whom. In the organisation, where hierarchy is amorphous, individual merit and the authority it wields is rightfully earned.

PLEASE ALLOW MYSELF TO MANAGE MYSELF

At its most rudimentary, *self-management* means companies without bosses. But what it's predicated on–trust, competence, and dignity–is much more revealing of the change in our approach to how work can get done.

Self-management is a deliberate choice adopted to help companies advance their mission. It's an ongoing experiment that evolves over time, much the same as people do. The practice helps workers feel comfortable with uncertainty, adopt a beginner's mindset, and strive to continuously improve. Perhaps most importantly, it provides the agency for workers to define how they work so they might discover meaning.

'In the past, you had control through compliance. In the future, you're going to have control through transparency, social pressure, and responsibility,' explains organisational designer Aaron Dignan. Like a two-way Uber review, you know your colleagues are performing at their peak and so you too seek to punch above your weight. And while it may not suit everyone, the benefits of self-management are hard to argue against: more engaged, happy, creative, and collaborative. Oh yes, let's not forget that self-managed organisations are way more efficient with at least a 35 percent boost to productivity.

Self-management cultures treat employees like adults so they can shape their own work. They freely collaborate with colleagues, manage their own time, and make conscious decisions on how to best contribute. This keeps employees engaged and provides a safe environment in which they can stand up and speak their mind. You're encouraged to be a shaper, you're expected to be you.

Focus on your strengths while cultivating new skills on the go. This was integral to the philosophy of Peter Drucker, the father of modern management. The best way to manage yourself is to know yourself. Indeed, you can't do what you love until you *know your own bone.*

This can mean tossing out the rule book and starting to do things as you see fit. This is quite possibly the unspoken reason you got hired in the first place. We're just at the beginning of the self-management wave. While companies like Buurtzorg may be blazing the way, the foundation has been decades in the making.

LET MY PEOPLE GO

In 1980, a newly appointed CEO of Brazilian manufacturer Semco Partners did something radical. The fresh-faced 21-year-old Ricardo Semler abruptly fired 60% of the top managers. This shaper then took a huge leap of faith by permitting staff to set their own hours. In an ultra-congested Sao Paulo, they could finally commute when traffic was lighter. More importantly, it sent a message: 'we trust you'.

Semler was championing self-management long before it was a 'thing'. At Semco, the sentiment 'get your work done and enjoy your life' is not a suggestion but a mandate. Semler foresaw that giving people more control over how they work not only helps them perform at their best, it also lets them understand and optimise the system of work that underpins the entire organisation. Under his leadership Semco grew from $4 million in revenue in 1982 to over $212 million in 2003. More impressively perhaps, is their employee turnover rates that have been less than one percent.

Today effective managers are a rare breed–only 1 out of every 10 have what it takes to be a courageous leader. Hence, a practice like self-management, that rids the business of managers altogether, has come into favour. Through the advice process, workers use their creativity and problem-solving abilities to do what they deem best.

And what might self-management look like with 70, 000 employees? A lot like Chinese consumer electronics company Haier. They've eliminated nearly 10,000 middle management positions and reorganised into an ecosystem of startups where employees function as entrepreneurs. Employees are active participants hungry to share risks and rewards. And as a result of this practice and other innovations in management and branding, the company has emerged from near bankruptcy to become one of the biggest appliance manufacturers in the world.

But what works for Buurtzorg, Semco, or Haier will not necessarily jive for others. Spotify has its unique brew of self-management and so does tomato processor Morning Star and blogging platform Medium. The point is to get inspired and borrow from self-management practices in a way that treats the organisation as an organism–responding to current needs as situations change. It's a recipe that should be modelled by others but made wholly their own.

There are several challenges to running a company with no bosses. When you can't hide from the truth, opinions, fears, and motivations are all exposed. This emotionally charged atmosphere can be both powerful and a drag. Workers who tend to bring their narrower professional selves to work aren't always game to bring their entire selves to the office. The vulnerability required isn't for the faint of heart–some don't want to deal with all the extra baggage when they get plenty of it at home.

The transition to a self-managed organisation can also be chock-full of hiccups. In 2013, when Zappos made the move to Holocracy (the former flag bearer of the self-management movement), 29% of the company's staff abandoned ship. This is the type of collateral damage that can be expected. So before implementing a self-management practice, it's imperative that all workers have elected to climb aboard. Only then can the organisation take advantage of processes and behaviours that respond well to changing winds. And as these practices gel, they form the breeze that wind that propels the company forward.

It's possible, heck it's even wonderful, to see discipline invoked in such a way as to free and empower people. And what this enables is good work, excellent service, fair prices, and strong financial performance to all coexist. Hands down, investing in people in this fashion leads to high performance.

CHOOSE YOURSELF

Edwin Jansen is a shaper. He is the Head of Marketing at Fitzii, a free, cutting edge hiring platform. Job titles don't mean much at his company since they eliminated managers in 2015. Different people step up to lead depending on the activity or project. No one has command over other team members and so hierarchy, by design, is dynamic. Distributed decision-making means leaving egos and positional authority at the door. Individual merit and the power it wields is rightfully earned.

'The individual needs to see that their success is going to be self-driven. I am going to pick myself, define what I want to do, what difference do I want to make, and how I will be valuable to people,' insists Jansen. He has learned to manage himself better and now helps other co-workers do the same. Everyone contributes their very best not because of a tyrant boss, but because they have the desire, control, and are aligned with Fitzii's mission.

Their teams work in parallel across product and development, sales and marketing, and human resources. Crucially, each plays a strategic planning role–taking responsibility for their own governance and for how they interact with other departments within the organisation. Since influence flows to the right people at the right time, roadblocks of middle management and office politics cease to exist.

While self-management can be a distinctive characteristic of an amorphous organisation, it's an *evolutionary purpose* that's the hallmark. Belgian author and politician Frédéric Laloux explains that companies like Fitzii, which he calls *teal organisations*, have an independent force that propels them. In other words, 'being your best' and doing work that matters only holds weight when the goal of the company is worthy. This is in stark contrast to the majority of today's corporations that still operate with machine-age practices where people are resources to be exploited and profit overshadows purpose.

In these kinds of supportive environments, shapers become wholehearted and rise up to challenges. Since moving to self-management, Fitzii generates more value for customers, staff, and partners. Ask others at software company Buffer or remote company Automattic about *choosing yourself* and they'll agree.

BLACK DUCKS AND OPEN NETWORKS

On the bleeding edge of the self-management movement are peer-to-peer (P2P) networks. In 2016, Black Duck Open Hub, which tracks open source projects, reported nearly 4 million contributors working on nearly 700,000 projects. Apache, a free open-source software, dwarfs Microsoft by powering half of all the world's web pages. Freelancers flex their muscles with Amazon Mechanical Turk, educators with Udemy, researchers with NineSigma, social innovators with OpenIDEO, creatives with Hit Record, entrepreneurs with Kickstarter, and anyone with the inclination and time on their hands, with Wikipedia. Whatever your poison, whether for pleasure or pay, there's likely a match just for you in the *platform economy*.

If you're running your own show, managing yourself can seem like no biggie. While this may be the case now, you will come to change over time and what you'll need will change as well. The incoming flood of independent workers will make more room for collaboration but also make a more competitive landscape.

Shapers need the confidence and competence to create value and get paid time and again.

Some in the gig economy will rely on the usual suspects like Uber and Etsy but many will depend on a new breed of upstarts. Mastering how to manage yourself will help safeguard against exploitative or overly precarious work. Portable benefits, compensation funds, and other schemes will continue to grow to help to mitigate risk, but it won't be enough. The onus will fall on independent workers to know how and when to plug into the right platforms.

Whether inside or outside of a company (and indeed this line continues to blur), knowing yourself will be essential. Self-cultivation–stretching your own mind and capacities–will be tantamount. And seeing the forest from the trees will enable you to view the entire system of work and your place within it. Ask yourself what is the one thing that you, and only you, can bring to the world? Shapers take a wide-angle worldview to build their tolerance and cultivate their talent. Together, by rehearsing and refining these practices, we refuse to cheat the world of our best contributions.

A WORKING PROTOTYPE

A self-managed company does not necessarily mean a chaotic one. 'It sounds like a crazy idea, but self-management is actually the solution to our most foundational problems in business today,' claims Jansen. In a self-managed environment, there is no pretending to work; you're your own boss and you'd be letting yourself down.

The biggest challenge in adopting self-management may rest in first daring to employ such a conscious practice. People generally resist change, and self-managed organisations are designed to anticipate and welcome change and to do so with open arms. Secondly, the work climate in these organisations is more authentic, requiring workers to confront obstacles and tensions head on. And finally, not everyone has the emotional stamina, or is even willing, to manage themselves with such fervour and fortitude.

Some workers won't jump at the chance to work in a setting that is constantly going to challenge them. Yet funnily enough, shapers follow their intuition and sense how and when to move into their stretch zone–because it's here where they keep the fire burning for their work.

Managing ourselves well means using our head (cognitively crafting our inner working life), hearts (catering to what truly motivates us), and hands (knowing when and how to direct our energy). It necessitates that we make really good decisions on how to structure our work in order to achieve what we intend.

What's needed then is to build courage, learn how to take responsibility, and experiment in order to lead yourself within a malleable organisational structure. Shapers must cultivate serious mental fitness, and be able to see themselves as a working prototype to continually improve upon. We are discerning in wielding influence within our networks. Indeed, we are complex adaptive systems, and self-management is a model purposefully created to harness more of our human capital in a time when we need it most.

To roll with the times, self-management will surely evolve into a hipper organising model. Whatever it may look like, the companies at this frontier will adhere to one tenet so simple yet too often ignored: it's humans that make the business. We may be imperfect beings, but we're inherently adaptive. And propelling us to achieve a five-star rating isn't such a bad thing after all.

CHAPTER 12

BACK TO SCHOOL WITHOUT THE BULL

We can view work for what it's becoming; an experimental practice to evolve. It occupies a psychological space as much as a physical one. The key is to know what to focus on at have the ability to do so. We need environments that allow for strong connections, learning and growth, and our values to be lived. The companies that get this create cultures that let individuals gel so they can do their very best work.

After World War II, East London never quite recovered like other parts of the city. Once a bustling fashion and textile district, it was littered with depressed and rundown buildings. In 2010, British delegates flew to Silicon Valley to do something about their problem. Riding on the coat-tails of the local startup scene, their big idea was to pitch East London as *Tech City*–a future startup Mecca.

After countless meetings with Silicon Valley investors, no one was taking the bait. Their last meeting with former Google CEO Eric Schmidt took a different turn. Just a few years after that meeting, the East London Google campus was buzzing. They would soon double down and expand the campus to accommodate 3,000 more Googlers. This set the stage for entrepreneurs to flood the city and help London become one of the best startup hubs in the world.

Unlike traditional businesses, campuses are dedicated places for creativity and experimentation. Sometimes parading as a PR stunt, the campus theme has found its way into plenty of organisations while taking on many guises. High-flying agencies tout their *creative labs*, hip venture capitalists their *investment studios*, and governments their *creative clusters*. They all are, or at least aspire to be, safe havens in which to fail.

Co-living may be the ultimate expression of extending college life into adulthood. These startups, ranging from glorified hostels to extravagant resorts, cater to an itinerant labour pool that seeks to work on the move. Whichever way it manifests, bringing the free-thinking campus mentality to the workplace is no fad. By design, they aim to provide the optimal conditions for rapid learning and innovation. And as we'll see in Chapter 14, becoming a learning organisaton is imperative to thrive in the future of work.

At its core, the campus concept is really a way to inspire a different attitude towards work. But employees must be aligned with their company's values to have any hope of feeling inspired and motivated. Shockingly, only one quarter of American employees believe in the values of their company. Workers continue to subordinate themselves to bureaucratic corporations in some way, every day, in order to do their job. No hipster office space nor snazzy perk will make up for the fact that a company's stated values don't hold water.

The Googleplex in Mountain View, California, was completed in 1996. Lego's campus in Denmark, completed a quarter of a century later, demonstrates the evolution. Made out of real-life Lego blocks, this wonder office can flex to fit pretty much any context. It's outfitted with a public park, rooftop garden, and golf course. Most notable is its emphasis on playfulness and collaboration while still catering to other modalities of work. Every mode of activity has its own dedicated floor.

LEGO Headquarters in Billund, Denmark.
Image courtesy of C.F. Møller Architects and LEGO.

MAKING WORK, WORK

One of the biggest obstacles to getting great work done may still be the physical office. Many of these dire places rob inhabitants of their focus (and soul for that matter), through a constant stream of distractions. If handed a magic wand, most employees would change their working environment so they could be more productive. Bold leaders appreciate the fine balance between people and place and cater to the variety of ways employees work.

A far-out vision for achieving this harmony in work could be that of architecture professor David Dewane. His *Eudaimonia Machine* (recall that eudaimonia means human flourishing) has the lofty goal of helping workers reach their full potential. Featuring a series of five distinct rooms, each is dedicated to a specific mode of work: the gallery for inspiration, the salon for conversation, the library for research, the office for light work, and my personal favourite, the chamber for deep work. There are no hallways so you move through each room, sequentially edging towards your most concentrated work. All that's missing, it seems, is a dedicated space to recharge, which may just really entail decamping from the office altogether to get some fresh air.

Gallery	Salon	Library	Office	Chamber
inspiration	conversation	research	light work	deep work

Entrance

Courtesy Amar Singh, Designer: www.ummerr.com.

Some firms hire architects, interior designers, workplace strategists, psychologists, and even mathematicians to design the perfect office for their particular needs. But in reality, work is something you feel empowered to do, not necessarily somewhere you need to be. The promise of fuelling creativity through space design is a nuanced one. That special something businesses are looking for–fostering the right energy–comes from people. And since humans, like businesses, evolve over time, healthy work environments need to change in concert with their occupants and the general state of the world. 'Those [firms] who get it right, attract, inspire and embrace growth gracefully,' says Oliver Marlow of architecture practice Tilt. The best workspaces in the future will place the highest priority on focus–optimising for workers to concentrate, contemplate, collaborate, and create.

The precise destination of work tomorrow, whether geographic or virtual, will be an arbitrary concern. Many companies have rid of the office altogether. Because great work can, and will, continue to happen online. Work happens in those temporal places that cater best to the technological, creative, and intellectual needs of the individual and team.

Automattic, the holding company behind blogging platform Wordpress.com is the darling example. Talk about efficiency: the business has under 1,200 employees yet astonishingly powers 37% of all sites on the web. CEO Matt Mullenweg declares, 'There are companies that are finding new ways to work, that allow people to set their own hours, have more flexibility, live wherever they want in the world and they're going to attract the best people.'

At one point Mullenweg's company had a plush office at Pier 38 in San Francisco's Embarcadero. It was only a five-minute walk from his apartment, but his preference, like many in the company, was to work from home. You bet they shut their office and the company continues to flourish. They're living proof that giving workers flexibility and control over their life works. Mullenweg continues, 'In the future, [companies] will either be distributed or be taken over by companies that are, because the smartest people in the world are going to want to work this way.'

Those shapers appreciate this already see work as a practice to experiment with depending on the *mode* of work, *moment* in time, or given *mood*. Recall a time when you were doing emails when you would have been better off preparing for a presentation? Or a time when you were slogging away on a project late at night when your brain was fried? Or showing up to do the work but just not feeling it? The point is that the 'place' in which the work happens is really any that fosters creativity, problem solving, and skills development.

THE MAGIC NUMBER

Gone are the days when employees were left clueless on how staff were treated. A new crop of services like Officevibe provide real-time metrics on company cultures. And a quick search on Glassdoor provides testimonials from former employees.

As it concerns what it's really like to work somewhere, business transparency is no longer a choice. Squarespace, the business highlighted earlier in the book, gets it right. Voted New York's best place to work countless times, their Manhattan office may be static, yet how they work is anything but. They live their values by respecting, inspiring, and challenging workers and encouraging them to be their most creative–wherever that may happen to be.

The larger than life personalities of founders can help shape a vibrant startup culture. But as businesses scale, it won't suffice on its own. Switched-on companies like W.L Gore & Associates (makers of Gore-Tex fabric) stick to the logic of the Dunbar number. They cap their departments at 150 people because, as humans, this is the maximum number of stable relationships that can be maintained at any one time.

One reason why midsize family businesses have flourished throughout history is because they remain nimble, typically less than 150 employees. There are therefore strong bonds and good communication between workers. It's these businesses that account for a whopping 60% of global employment. Military units are often capped at this magic number too–when lives are on the line, it's helpful if everyone knows each other's name.

You can't design culture, not intelligently at least. It manifests through the conversations that occur between employees, cus-tomers, suppliers, partners, and anyone and everyone who comes into contact with your company.

'Culture is the invisible glue that holds everything together in the equation of professional life,' says shaper and Facebook community partner, Victoria Stoyanova. Without this glue working, things don't just fall apart, they fail to stick together in the first place.

For too many, there's a disconnect between the company culture that managers first set then strive to realise, and the culture they experience every day when they come into work. When there isn't a clear goal or a shared language, it's difficult for a culture to gel.

Cultivating a resilient company culture means truly understanding the ongoing interplay of worker bees within a

> The best place to work isn't a place after all; it's a state of mind.

complex system. It requires workers to have the tools and the support they need to thrive. Turns out, the best place to work isn't a place after all; it's a state of mind.

CHAPTER 13

TOOLS TO HELP YOU SUCCEED

The way we're working isn't working. Shapers do their best work by managing their energy and attention as well as setting clear goals and boundaries. We need to use technology as a tool and not a diversion. And when we reveal those rituals of work that serve us, it's crucial that we cultivate them.

Neil Wilks is a Brit in New York who hasn't lost his love of tea. Each weekday morning, this shaper rises at 6.30 and with cuppa in hand lazes about the kitchen table. His calm surroundings put him in a well chirpy mood. Perusing emails on his smartphone, he uses this particular device because it evokes brevity.

Wilks started out in the world of human resources back when it was dubbed 'personnel'. He cut his teeth building resilient company cultures at Nokia, Cisco, Amazon, Soundcloud, and Meetup. It's the freedom to choose where and how to work that underpins his working style. 'It's about finding different environments to keep myself stimulated. And, I'm an old guy, right? So many people are much younger than me and much more flexible in their working styles,' confesses the vibrant 52-year-old.

Once out the door, Wilks hops on the J Line to Manhattan and switches to his iPad. The confines of the train (in particular the intermittent internet) provide time for more thoughtful work. This *found* time is sacred for him. In today's knowledge economy, it's all about moving and grooving with your mood. You match your deskspace to your headspace and seek out the most nourishing environment to rock the particular task at hand. 'I like to be able to come and go [to the office] as I please. I like the security of a home base, but I don't need a personal space–I just need my flock. If I've got my flock I'm happy,' Wilks remarks. And for many in his flock, this freedom in work has become the norm.

Moving and grooving with your mood means matching your deskspace to your headspace and seeking out the most nourishing environment to rock the particular task at hand.

Wilks's weekend work routine is a tad more relaxed yet still resembles the workweek. He moves fluidly between locations and tasks–planning, reading, designing, and tapping away effortlessly on the go. He shifts his thinking by dropping himself into a different environment and switching between devices. An average weekend might involve working *1 hour in front of the TV (smartphone), 4 hours in the car (tablet), and 1.5 hours on the train (laptop).* That totals nearly a full day of work over the weekend in periodic bursts that suit his temperament.

This kind of *burst working* can be delightful on those days when the rest of the world isn't working. And while some may pity those like Wilks who toil away over the weekend, he's doing so by design. For many, the weekend is the most productive and creatively rewarding time, largely indistinguishable from the workweek.

The pace of Wilks's working style is distinctively rhythmic so as to keep his flow. It lets him excel at his job, which is helping others be their very best. 'Forty-hour work weeks are a relic of the Industrial Age. Knowledge workers function like athletes–train and sprint, then rest and reassess,' declares AngelList founder, Naval Ravikant.

Discovering and safeguarding his time to do and be his best is what distinguishes people like Wilks from the rest of the pack.

Swedish psychologist K. Anders Ericsson, best known for his research on experts, found that what separates stand-out musicians, artists, chess players, and others is not just how long and hard they practise–but *how they train*. Peak performers punch 60–90 minutes of highly focused training, immediately followed by short breaks. And, crucially, the maximum amount of focused attention these high performers are capable of in a day is four and a half hours.

Computer scientist Cal Newport's *Deep Work* popularised this research. Newport urges us to take on cognitively demanding activities in a completely distraction-free state. Switching on for intense bursts of this deep work and then shifting into a more restorative gear can boost creativity and performance.

In contrast to deep work is the lighter stuff. These are tasks you can perform with less concentration and often using little brainpower. Think of the better part of your email regimen, syncing your calendar with meetings, grooming your to-do list, catching up on articles online, or pruning your social media accounts. In this light work, you can be open and responsive to the world while still making headway. The trick here is to intentionally batch your work into deep and light categories and keep them wholly distinct from one another. Like oil and water, they just don't mix.

WHAT COLOUR IS MY CLOCK?

Knowing your biological clock, or *chronotype,* is also essential for doing great work. Like all living organisms, our bodies are governed by the same physiological principles in a 24-hour rhythm. You might think you're an early bird or night owl but it's more than likely you're somewhere in the middle–a third bird. This means you'll experience those dreaded afternoon dips sometime between 2 and 3 pm. The goal is to do your most challenging and important work when you're most energised. Since your circadian rhythms are uniquely yours, you need to tweak them so you regularly hit your stride in your *golden hours.* Simply knowing when you should and shouldn't work is a sure-fire way to peak performance.

How might we create habits that make space for more eureka moments? The short answer is through more 'brain blinks'. 'There's a great deal of distracting visual stimuli streaming into the brain all the time, and minimizing that helps us devote more energy to an immediate task,' explains John Kounios, professor of applied cognitive and brain sciences at Drexel University. In geek speak, a burst of alpha-waves in the brain is dialing down all that buzzing activity in your noggin and 'blinks' right before you have a big insight. This is part of the reason why we do some of our very best thinking in the shower. 'There's sensory restriction–white noise and you can't really see much,' continues Kounios. It's also why you might look up at the ceiling or close your eyes when trying to think deeply. By refusing to focus on anything in particular, we can gleefully push our creative envelope.

Maybe it's meditation that can help unlock more. Don't worry if you're not a professional meditator, by no means am I trying to convert you–not just yet. You can run lo-fi and practise being present in the form of the pause. Several times throughout the day, take a minute or two and vacate everything. Try the 4-4-4 breathing technique. It's simple, it's powerful, and even Navy Seals do it to chill out.

➤ *Inhale through your nose for 4 seconds.*

➤ *Hold your inhale at the top for 4 seconds.*

➤ *Exhale through your mouth for 4 seconds.*

➤ *Rest for 4 seconds and then start again.*

➤ *Repeat the cycle for as many times as you fancy.*

You might be hopping out of your car or about to jump into another meeting–but before you do, stop as if the world were frozen. Try the exercise if it feels right–what happens next might surprise you. Obviously do not operate heavy machinery when trying this technique.

'Meditation is by far the most straightforward way to improve your concentration: a few minutes a day with your eyes closed, paying attention to the sensations of the breath in the nostrils, is the attentional equivalent of a decent workout at the gym,' explains time management myth-buster Oliver Burkeman. Should you fall asleep during your mini-meditation, that's OK–short naps are a great way to get a second wind of creative juice during the day. But assuming you don't nod off, come back to your breath. Chances are you'll be able to see the exact same thing in a whole new light.

Perhaps you need something else to get your mojo firing. A more apt hack for mind wandering may be a moving meditation. A much-loved one is putting one foot in front of the other. Aristotle loved walking. So did Charles Darwin. Poet and Novelist Helen Dunmore said long walks were the ultimate way for her to crystallise ideas. One of the main reasons walking is so powerful is because your inner world quietens and the world around you opens up. You give your mind a chance to reflect, integrate, and ruminate. You find that the problems that once had you stuck do so no longer.

A wandering mind is actually our brain's *default state*–where it chooses to go when we have nothing else to focus on. Shapers are serious about flexing the three pounds between their ears to dream up wild scenarios and as such are mindful to set the right conditions. And if walking isn't your bag, yoga, running, swimming, or even bathing could do. These activities, or non-activities if you will, let you tend to your body so that your cognitive brain can take a well-deserved break. Your subconscious mind gets a turn, affording you a new lens through which to see yourself and your work. You gain clarity on how to best exert your energy, reduce feelings of time scarcity, and stimulate your creativity.

BURST WORKING

At software business DeskTime employees are monitored (yes, it's a little Big Brother-ish) to understand precisely how top performers behave. They work in set intervals–switching between bursts of focused work sprinkled with short breaks. Bursts last around 52 minutes and rest periods about 17 minutes. While everyone has their distinct working style, it's by managing energy in this deliberate fashion that one can seriously optimise workflow.

Your rhythms of work are how you get stuff done–your particular habits and routines. Moving gracefully between bursts, resting, and lighter work is a result of superior self-management skills. But it's your rituals of work that bear the real significance. They hold your aspirations overhead and are symbolic of why you do what you do. While Dickens had a rhythm of walking up to 20 miles a day to let his mind wander, his ritual for working was much more finicky. He required absolute silence with nine particular objects on his window-facing desk, including a vase of fresh flowers, a gilt leaf with a rabbit perched upon it, and a bronze statuette of a gentleman embracing a swarm of puppies.

To ensure he's firing on all cylinders so he can help others, Neil Wilks ensures that he regularly refuels. His underlying concern for the welfare of his flock is also self-serving: when they soar, he soars. This is the deep well from which he derives his vitality and my guess is that this, more than anything, is what keeps him feeling and looking so youthful.

Discovering *when*, *where*, and *how* you work best really does take work. Some offices can actually be hostile environments for thoughtful work, where it feels next to impossible to get on with what you need to do. You need to therefore design the right conditions for performing at your peak. Creating this space that respects your mental energy will take discipline, craftiness, and training. But as your unique rhythms and rituals gel over time you'll find the rewards include more ingenuity, clearer thinking, and better outcomes.

And as you and your work evolve, you'll do regular check-ups, experiment from time to time, and tweak accordingly. Like a surfer navigating waves, these modalities of work require patience and persistence. It's an exercise in temperament. But it'll help create a sense of meaning and may just be your only saviour in a world screaming for your attention.

EMAIL HEAVEN OR HELL?

Email can be a real drag in our working lives. A blessing in some instances–but, for many, email inflicts more harm than good. Too often we forget these communications occur asynchronously to real life. And just because we can always be accessible, doesn't mean we should be. Some of the most prolific creators carefully limit both the frequency and the time they spend doing email.

We now spend over 60% of the workweek doing email or searching the web. By God, one UK study reports that an average British worker thinks doing four hours of email is a productive day at work. If you're a typical office worker, by bedtime, you'll have processed 124 emails. Everywhere one looks, a notification of some kind is lurking around the corner. I tend to think of email as a nasty habit like smoking. Arguably it's even more toxic when you consider the second-hand smoke emitted in the form of unsolicited communication, spam, and the carbon copy.

If by the off chance you're an email *Filer* (relying on ingenuity to create folders and file emails accordingly), you might consider switching teams to be a *Searcher* (relying on your worthy computer to do the 'filing' for you). On average, finding an email by searching happens 41 seconds faster than trying to dig it out from a folder. Now I'm sure your superior filing habits give you peace of mind and let you sleep like a baby at night–but it's not a long-term effective strategy. *Searchers* who rely on software are winning the battle against email. Like it or not, having faith in artificial intelligence in this respect will catapult you light-years ahead in 'crushing email'.

All those texts, DMs, emails, and all those snazzy notifications that flood in even as you read this very sentence aren't screaming for an immediate response (and now that I've got you thinking about it–don't you even dare). You can get to them on your own time, I promise they will still be there. Some of the happiest people I know disabled notifications on their smartphones years ago. With time and practice, shapers tame the craving to respond to the world while pushing their creativity to the max.

Of American smartphone users aged 18–44, 80% check their device first thing in the morning–moving into a reactive mode from the get-go. The pithy excuse is that the phone functions as the alarm. But what can also occur is a toxic wiring of the brain: triggering messages, dreadful news feeds, overwhelming bottomless social media 'updates', and analytics of snoring and fart patterns from last night's sleep. The easy hack is to buy an alarm clock.

We should not let our smart devices outsmart us–like beautifully designed handcuffs providing endless opportunities to waste time. A new and more responsible technology regimen is urgently needed. Technology should play the role of a great liberator, connecting us to the world on our own terms.

There is plenty of time (unless you're a surgeon or some other professional who works within life–death parameters) to respond to the world after breakfast, after accomplishing one of the priorities you intentionally set out to do. If you already do this, then good on ya. If you have young kids, I wish you luck. Consider involving them in some way (maybe set them up at a 'workstation' and practice the pomodor technique with them once a week). Or once you've spent some time with them or they are out the door, grab those 25-minutes for yourself. No kids? Find a buddy and try this out with them for at least one week–then reflect not just on what you got done, but how you feel about it.

HARD-BOILED BOUNDARIES

On New Year's Day, without fail, John Grisham starts writing a new book. Five days a week, each morning at 7 am, he's in the same room, sitting in the same chair, tapping away on his same old trusty computer, and most importantly, with the same cup full of coffee. No beeps, pings, messaging, or internet for that matter–absolutely no distractions. And like clockwork, six months later he's finished and out pops his new book. He's been doing this for over 30 years. You can do the maths to see how many books that makes.

While we might not all need to be this regimented, discovering and safeguarding time is absolutely essential to doing your best work. Shapers schedule uninterrupted time for when they hit a stride, permitting them to indulge in moments of optimal performance while they're truly performing. To succeed in today's constantly pinging world, we too must protect our most creative times to ensure we keep our flow.

Grisham's success as a novelist is no doubt aided by his uncompromising regimen. He's a remarkable writer, but his work ethic is also nothing short of remarkable. Long before time blocking was even a thing, Grisham was batching his time. Prior to him becoming a full-time novelist, he got up at 5 am to write before heading off to try cases as a lawyer. How's that for a side hustle?

At one point in time we didn't have this endless stream of distractions. Attention wasn't a commodity and busyness wasn't a bragging right. Our love affair with productivity wasn't so fierce and our obsession with consuming things, well, wasn't an obsession. The advertising machine didn't exacerbate a continuous feeling of 'lacking stuff' and neither Instagram nor Netflix tempted us every waking hour. God knows the cards are stacked against us today for expediting doing good work.

*At one point in time we didn't have this endless stream of distractions.
Attention wasn't a commodity and busyness wasn't a bragging right.*

One way to overcome all the noise is to set clear-eyed boundaries. In response to constant digital noise, some individuals temporarily quit social media while others, like Maneesh Sethi, go to crazy extremes–deliberately employing someone to slap him whenever he tries to check his Facebook feed. The point is that focus is now the holy grail and we need to sharpen our attention span in order to work deeply and purposefully.

Still others use a wee bit of *obstacle thinking*. Creativity expert Jocelyn K. Glei explains that we can pursue our goals with more tenacity by imagining the obstacles in advance. In other words, before you get started, picture the challenges between your vision (whether that be finishing a blog post or launching a new venture) and reality. When these obstacles do arise, they'll be less intimidating.

Glei has been perfecting how she works for over a decade. She plans her projects around cascading levels of attention. She might have a primary project like an online course and a secondary one like a screenplay. When she turns up to do the work that's in pole position, if she's just not feeling it, she can revert to the more indulgent project. Glei also presents a compelling case for productivity where, from time to time, we should frankly just fuck off.

Indeed, all this burst working requires that we decamp and give our noggins a well-deserved break. We have cleverly managed to backpedal to a constant state of hyper attention, always on the lookout for the next dopamine hit. The deep attention required to read a book like this has become all too rare.

Shapers kick-start their day the right way–giving themselves space and time–turning the tables on being overly responsive and setting the expectations of others to respect their work rhythms. They experiment with and tame technology, so it best serves them. When it gets to the nitty gritty, shapers consciously use technology as a tool, rather than a diversion. They then find themselves finishing, if not a novel per year, at least those endeavours that hold the most meaning.

BUSY NOT PRODUCTIVE

Computing power today enables us to complete the equivalent of a full 1970s workday in just one and a half hours. Breakthroughs in microchip technology have caused productivity to more than triple since economist John Maynard Keynes predicted the shorter workweek nearly a hundred years ago. Surely he'd be rolling over in his grave to learn how ineptly we work, and more to the point, how we squander the precious time we could otherwise enjoy.

The advent of technology was supposed to provide us with more time for leisure. So what gives? For one thing, we toil more fervently to contain our fears of not having, or being, enough. While modern technologies have made work infinitely easier, we have created the implicit pressure to work more. We work harder than any previous generation to amass more stuff that we can't find the time to use.

The average full-time American clocks 47 hours a week. While the demand for knowledge-based work escalates, our daily cap for cognitively taxing work remains the same at four and a half hours a day. If we aren't able to work smarter naturally, surely there is a way to hack it! So we slurp coffee, pop pills, and listen to our audiobooks at 2x speed. We remain busy but not necessarily productive. Our devices keep us tied to our employers at all hours not by mandate, but often because we just can't help ourselves.

To further compound the problem: despite the awesome power at our fingertips, we're just not that effective in how we work. As we've seen, the office itself can be such a spirit-sapping place–it's a miracle anything gets done. It's all too easy for lazy workers to pretend to be busy. They train to become masters at the art of not working, at work.

If only our relationship with technology, especially of the digital variety, weren't so complicated. It has become the double-edged sword–both our best friend and worst enemy.

There's a better way. Shapers first acknowledge that the way we're working, isn't working. We see this as a ripe opportunity to renew ourselves, redesign our work, and reinvent our organisations. And we surely benefit from contemporary practises to help us navigate to a desirable future. So we now turn to five principles to help us do just that.

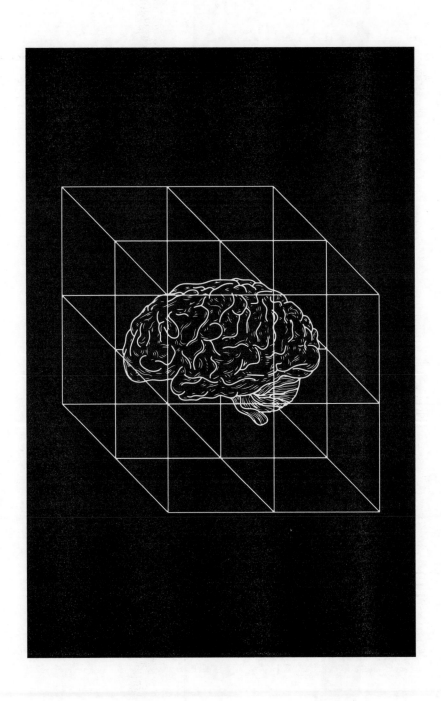

PART III

PRINCIPLE FOR THE FUTURES OF WORK

Abundance is not about providing everyone on this planet with a life of luxury–rather it's about providing all with a life of possibility.

—Peter Diamandis

The future of work is about the meaning we find within it. There are many possible futures on the horizon and predicting just one isn't all that useful. Instead, we can set our sights on a preferable future where we better balance the marriage between humans, technology, and the planet. To help navigate there, shapers adopt the principles of Learning, Feeling, Leading, Becoming and Futuring.

CHAPTER 14

LEARNING: WONDER AT WORK

Education is what's done to you while learning is what you do to yourself. Progressive companies place less value on degrees and formal education may even be a liability. What matters is just how damn good you are and your potential to learn to change and become even better.

Reflecting back to Saturday 23, November 1963, Lyndon B. Johnson confessed, 'You don't learn anything when you're talking'. It was the day after John F. Kennedy's assassination, and Johnson was thrust into the presidency. He was bright enough to admit what he didn't know–and at such a delicate time, wise enough to listen attentively to those around him.

There are countless theories on how people learn but most would agree, is that everyone favours a different learning style. You might prefer to go it alone rocking an audio book on a power walk. Perhaps it's immersing in a group exercise that's your bag. Maybe you can often be found hanging out in a buzzy cafe reading or in a quiet space feverishly writing. If you're more somatic in style, we might see you pacing about looking like you're talking to yourself as you commit things to memory. Or like many, maybe you love to geek out over diagrams, charts, and visual eye candy. You get the picture.

One inescapable truth of how we effectively learn is through imitation. It's how we act and the stories we share that enable us to make progress. So what we really mean when we say a company has a great culture is that the established behaviour resonates with us. Shapers model new and better ways of work and as such have influence over how the culture evolves.

Like President Johnson, perhaps the most powerful way to learn in a professional setting is by listening. Too many people seem to be enamoured with hearing the sound of their own voice. But when we talk, we're often just repeating what we already know. No one knows it all, and even in those instances when we think we do, we can still choose to chow some humble pie. Pleasant surprises usually await.

When we learn through active listening we get outside of our own heads, stretch our minds, and widen our perspectives. If we manage to completely focus our listening, we clue up to those unsaid things like body language and tone of voice. There's so much colour we can soak up from our fellow yappers. Whichever way you fancy gathering, processing, and sharing information, it's important to remember the learning psychology at play in your day to day.

Now suppose that all of our workplaces doubled as classrooms. They are spaces where it's OK to fail and where you're at ease being your fallible self. It's safe to try things out and you're encouraged to follow your nose. There is no judgement for any errors so long as you learn from them. There's rich cognitive diversity and contrasting ways of working make for an electric environment. The office–physical or virtual–is a breeding ground for innovation. As you test new ideas and approaches to your work, you're supported to grow with regular and constructive feedback. Sounds like an ideal scenario from a Brené Brown talk, right?

MOONSHOTS AND BARGAIN BIN LEARNING

Self-dubbed 'moonshot factory', Google's X is famous for turning zany ideas into reality. They design kites to generate electricity and create next generation drones to deliver packages. Captain of X, Astro Teller, appreciates that in order to fuel innovation, you have to design an 'emotional path of least resistance'. Mistakes are your friends and failure is unabashedly rewarded. The company is famous for applauding colleagues when they screw up.

A shared understanding at X is that leaving the good behind means creating bandwidth to pursue the great. Perhaps the aptly named *Project Loon* epitomised this. The idea of building massive stratospheric balloons to bring Wi-Fi to the rest of the world was first thought to be totally ridiculous. But it's precisely this try-it-out-and-see-what-we-learn kind of culture that took this loony idea from sticky note to the sky.

To be sure, we can't all work at Google's X, nor can many companies operate with the same opulent mandate. But we certainly can mimic the spirit of a workplace that's an engine for learning.

The bedrock of any *learning organisation* is its ability to cultivate an environment that is highly conducive to learning. By effect, this permits the organisation to transform itself, according to systems scientist Peter Senge. Indeed, our world is just one big lab and our organisations are experiments we're running within it. If our organisations aren't evolving, then neither are we. As our work grows to become more opaque, it's the companies that learn to foster and reinforce learning that will blaze the trail towards innovation.

Our education system is a direct by-product of the industrial age. Traditionally, we think of education as something that happens before one goes to work. Remember Manny? His plan was linear: go to school, skill up, and then set off on his career. But learning is nuanced and wholly dependent on the situation and cultural context of the learner. We all have different learning styles and, more to the point, like Manny we have varying motivations in why we seek to level up in the first place. Trumping that of any other workforce strategy is enabling workers to reskill, according to the World Economic Forum.

> As our work grows to become more opaque, it's the companies that learn to foster and reinforce learning that will blaze the trail towards innovation.

To be certain, rote learning worked well in the machine age. Many of the luxuries we enjoy today would not exist were it not for the industrial era's decree for progress. The work centred around synchronising, standardising, and maximising for productivity. Productivity was (and in many ways still is) measured by the straightforward correlation between labour and financial return. The problem, of course, is that we don't live in this era anymore. Maximising worker well-being through learning isn't some fluffy pipe dream–it's an urgent as well as smart business strategy.

Operating workers as machines, or *mechanomorphism* as it's known, is just lame. That Smithian hypothesis that we must be managed as resources is giving way to hard science: humans are assets to be set free. While hip businesses have evolved to meet the truth behind human motivation, most still run on legacy systems. But perks and benefits can only go so far. The upgrade we desperately need includes installations of inspiration, flexibility, and self-cultivation. We all want the ability to think on our feet and continuously improve. Indeed, 'If you can't learn, you can't thrive', claims computer scientist Cal Newport.

> While hip businesses have evolved to meet the truth behind human motivation, most still run on legacy systems. The upgrade we desperately need includes installations of inspiration, flexibility, and self-cultivation.

Working with what we know and can learn, or knowledge work as it's become known, is ambiguous by nature. The better we can execute *while* learning, the better we can create, produce, and innovate. This requires us to take ownership of our own means of production.

Shapers habitually show up to do the work in order to fuel, train, and stretch their brains. It's quantity of output that eventually leads to quality. In principle we can grasp this, but to muster the willpower to create and stick to an enduring practice is a whole different story.

To cater to the *learning by doing* modality it helps to understand your unique talents, how to build on them, as well as develop new skills. Again, the most

> To constantly fuel, train, and stretch our brains, shapers habitually show up to do the work.

valuable asset an organisation has is its people. Never designed with this in mind, most companies fail epically here. Companies at the frontier are positioned there for a reason: they lay fertile ground for people to become better workers and better versions of themselves.

When change is accelerating at unparalleled speeds and everyone around you is busy doing stuff, it's very easy to feel like a bystander. But the real benefit of doing, is learning. Switched-on businesses commonly view failure as a 'bargain-priced learning opportunity' explain Joi Ito and his collaborator Jeff Howe in their book *Whiplash*. Google's X goes a step further by rewarding failure–a practice that runs counter to the productivity mandate of the past century.

THE WOLF YOU FEED

It seems like a no brainer but it's so often something we neglect: if you want your performance to soar, you need to cater to how you learn best. You must directly apply learning to your own lived experience. Duo lingo might help you grasp rudimentary Spanish, but it's only a complement to the direct learning that takes place through jamming with a Spaniard. Meaningful learning only happens when we picture ourselves in a future scenario putting insights into action. 'Study without desire spoils the memory, and it retains nothing that it takes in,' wrote Leonardo da Vinci. Our minds favour challenges so long as they are tied to our intrinsic motivations. Indeed, as aspiring shapers we can catapult ahead when we learn how to learn how to change.

Every day, we self-select the material that is most interesting and relevant to our given situation. We have become expert curators of our personal learning systems, working tirelessly to convert information into tacit skills and knowledge so we can 'perform'. Learners who favour reading know this all too well. If only the dynamics at work were as evident. People so often don't share the valuable information they could or, when they do communicate, they don't say what they mean. Our workplaces force us to constantly read between the lines.

Letting destructive behaviour fester, Tony Schwartz learned his lesson the hard way. A leading expert on employee performance, Schwartz explains that leaders have a significant impact on the mood of others simply by virtue of their authority. When Schwartz made a poor hire, the venom of the new employee infected the whole organisation until that employee was terminated. 'I'd allowed myself to be unduly influenced by a destructive kind of energy, and then I had unconsciously communicated that energy to others,' confesses Schwartz. When our abilities to be intellectually nourished and express ourselves are fettered, it may have a cataclysmic effect.

When we lead from hurt rather than heart, as shame expert Brené Brown explains, 'We're working our shit out on other people'. If we want to turn the tables, we need to start by changing ourselves. The unresolved issues we all have inside are not for our colleagues to sort out. It's only when we recognise and accept the source of our regressed behaviour that we can rise to express our authentic selves. By journeying deep down into the dark basement of our souls, we encounter our fragility and face our fears. Only then do we begin to build the courage to create new possibilities. The choice is ours to express ourselves and reach different outcomes. And if we fail to get to the root of the pain and the resulting behaviour, instead of a one-time kinda thing, it becomes chronic.

Just like a scene out of 'The Office', you may be unruffled and see the humour in the childish behaviour exhibited by your colleagues. Instead of it being frustrating, you see it as brilliant entertainment. OK that's probably a stretch. The point is that most workplaces are simply not designed to cater to our intellectual, physical, emotional, and spiritual needs. In a Harvard Business Review study of 20,000 employees around the world, a whopping 60% said that their companies were not meeting a single one of these needs.

When we show care, competence, and courage it sets a blueprint for others to internalise and emulate. When we tolerate power plays, scheming, sabotage, lying, contempt, and aggression, it creates a culture that sways in a different direction. We saw how workers imitate one another, so toxic behaviour can spread like wildfire. Everything comes down to the wolf we decide to feed.

'The key for organisations is to make it just as easy and effective to learn new skills inside the organisation as it is to do so outside the organisation,' explains author Daniel Pink. Until we reinvent our workplaces to be safe spaces in which to learn from trial and error, we will continue to stifle both innovation and the human spirit.

In work cultures that are resistant to change, an appetite for experimentation resembles driving the wrong way on a one-way street. Learning something new and useful on the job and then being disempowered to implement it leads to frustration, resentment, or backlashing. When failure is taboo, employees suffer.

Experimentation without learning isn't only a waste, it harms a company when compounded over time. But when leaders help their teams see mistakes as learnings, insights can be integrated to form better working practices and more wholehearted workplaces. It all starts with baby steps that give workers the confidence and comfort to try. There is no foolproof prescription, bar asking: is this effort safe to try? Does it facilitate learning? And are we equipped to do something valuable with the insights we've gained?

PLAY TO SLAY AT WORK

LEGO gets it. The wonder of their campus has made their *ways of working* the stuff of legend. The toy manufacturer is not only a learning organisation where it's safe to fail, they purposefully inject playfulness into the office–a quality integral to creativity.

Hub experience manager Catherine Dernulc explains that workers can feel anxious and stressed in environments where it's taboo to fail. 'With stress, you lose your creativity. So now we try it and if it fails, 'well, let's see what we can do with it'–and we have these iterations.' LEGO is built on a culture of trust and freedom. The company isn't just building bricks, they're building work so it gets better all the time.

Indeed, as we ourselves change, so will our approach to work. When we make space for self-cultivation, we nourish both ourselves and those around us. We move into that stretch zone to raise our capacities. Over time we witness the collective spirit soar–like compound interest for the soul. Shapers refuse to compromise in workplaces that stifle their growth. They'll adapt to make work better simply by giving *the new* a chance.

CHANGING EDUCATION AND LEARNING HOW TO CHANGE

Thriving in the future of work is not about the skills your team has right now but about the ones they can develop. Learning how to learn is the uber skill. We will need fortitude to change our workplaces so they house better stories for others to imitate and emulate. By modelling our institutions on classrooms we unleash an emotional contagion–perpetually learning and growing to be better.

Our education system has a long way to go to better equip future generations for the new world of work. Sure, progressive schools that practice 'personalised learning' are numerous in Scandinavia. Massive Open Online Courses (MOOCs) crossed the 100 million students mark in 2018 and virtual learning will continue to grow. But these are only partial band-aids to a much wider systemic problem.

Modelled on industrial age needs for units of productivity, education was designed in the image of the machine. Just as they signified the shift was over for the factory worker, bells indicate it's time to dash off to the next class. Students are synchronised by age and tests are standardised from curriculums set in stone. Learners are expected to store information deposited into them by their teachers like an ATM without the ability to recall and apply it directly to their own situations. This *banking* concept of education is wholly inadequate for capable learners in today's connected economy.

We first need to undo decades of institutionalised behaviour reinforced by parents, schools, and businesses. 'A lot of our cultural scripts for how to become successful are stuck on the older pattern of learning to do a job once and then having that career for the rest of your life, rather than continual learning,' says author of *Ultralearning* Scott Young. In the future of work, 'We will have new and interesting challenges throughout our career rather than decades of merely doing the same thing,' he continues. This is precisely why experiential and situational learning is so pervasive today.

The new education paradigm requires every child to have their own creativity nurtured, unique skills developed, and minds continually nourished. Students need to be armed with growth mindsets, can-do attitudes, emotional intelligence, self-confidence, and the versatility to learn on the fly. As they mature and enter the workforce, in addition to hard skills, they'll need superior time, energy, and self-management capabilities.

Instead of suppressing talent, we must nurture it. Every child needs to be challenged and supported to reach their potential. Clustering students by their age is arbitrary, adhering to curriculums that are often outdated before they are implemented is ineffective, and failing to understand how a given student learns best is tantamount to stifling their growth and creativity.

We don't know how the future will play out. But it's 'education that's meant to take us into this future that we can't grasp' declares creativity expert Sir Ken Robinson in the most widely viewed TED talk of all time. 'I believe our only hope for the future is to adopt a new conception of human ecology, one in which we start to reconstitute our conception of the richness of human capacity. Our education system has mined our minds in the way that we've strip-mined the earth, for a particular commodity, and for the future, it won't serve us. We have to rethink the fundamental principles on which we are educating our children,' he continues.

The population of the world continues to explode (it's estimated we will be upward of 10.5 billion earthlings by 2040), and more students are graduating from high school and college than ever before. Education reform is vital. The transformative influence of technology on work requires a shared understanding of what human intelligence really means and how it's best applied. It must build upon what we already know about intelligence, which is that it's diverse, dynamic, and distinct. Well-nourished through proper education, future generations may remark upon the coming decades as the learning revolution.

THE FINAL EXAM

Our organisations are failing us because they're not designed to function as engines for learning. Employees should get paid for both their intellectual property and what it is they'll need to know. But what we have, sadly, are corporations that reward conformity over professional growth.

Our education system is rooted in standardisation and mass synchronisation but will only sprout through personal, situational, and reflective practice. While the incoming workforce is being prepped for jobs that will soon be extinct, what they desperately need is the ability to learn how to learn.

As a young person, you're not allowed to sit out the future. You must cultivate a growth mindset. Future shapers will be given the leeway for cross-domain thinking and creative problem-solving. As we've seen, this is the modus operandi for both LEGO and Google X. Indeed, Google reports that Gmail, Google Maps, and

Adsense are all achievements born out of their creatively liberating practices. Those companies that liberate workers so they can follow their nose really know what's up.

Progressive organisations are adamant in promoting experimentation and playfulness–because that's where creativity resides. Providing safe spaces to have a little fun is a smart strategy. And cultivating curiosity isn't just trendy–it's winning the innovation game.

CHAPTER 15

FEELING: AN EMOTIONAL REVOLUTION

We abandoned the virtues of being, thinking, and feeling in favour of doing. If we want to better align our intention with action, we desperately need to rebalance the scales. After centuries of suppressing and neglecting our innermost thoughts and feelings, we yearn to return to a more natural and equable state.

We are human beings, not human doings. It's so easy to forget that. After the Age of Enlightenment in the 18th century, we became enamoured with acting in the world. But ain't no stopping us now–we've simply got too much invested. Our identities and sense of self-worth are enmeshed with the principles of making progress. And with our fixation on doing, comes the productivity ninjas and struggle pornographers we so cherish today.

We've neglected the 'Version of the self that's the opposite of the personal brand, one that not only resists appropriation but is too emergent and shape-shifting to be pinpointed,' says author of *How to Do Nothing,* Jenny Odell. Shifting into a slower gear means facing our fear of idleness. We forget how rare and valuable it is to do *nothing* from time to time. As a result, thinking and feeling play second fiddle to *doing.*

The industrial boom led to public schooling, life-extending antibiotics, and blueberries all year round. It also brought e-cigarettes, selfie-sticks, and McChickens. While we gorge on media and meat, we've become both physically and digitally obese. We've scorched the earth and our senses in a fashion that's unsustainable. We're precarious postmodernists because we indulge in indulgence. Somewhere along the road to *eudaimonia,* we've missed a beat.

Without the feeling of making progress–that intangible reward for our efforts–the workplace will continue to be an unhappy place. It's alarming how many can't see their contribution in their own work. The sheer scale of modern industries robs them of their sense of meaning. It's challenging to feel you're making a real difference when you're in a conglomerate of 100,000 employees. Weeks, months, or even years can zip by without having experienced the joy from making a difference in the lives of others. The system feels contaminated while the needle of progress never seems to move one iota.

We also know that beyond basic financial security, worker happiness doesn't increase with more pay and perks. Still, we want more and work harder. Slicker clothes, faster cars, and fancier vacations are just within reach. It's tiring keeping up with the Joneses when they keep moving into a splashier house.

Our feelings have also been assaulted by the advertising industrial complex for the better part of a century. Amassing more stuff and a higher status have come at a cost to the richness of our relationships. When we feel empty inside, the quick fix is to buy more. Consumer psychology and persuasive technology have come together in a deadly mix that makes us not just want more, but 'need' those things we didn't even know we wanted. Thrust by the Internet, there's no damn off button in our always-on, readily available, perpetually productive, and consumptive culture. Modesty and moderation appear laughable

> It's tiring keeping up with the Joneses when they keep moving into a splashier house.

aspirations in the Western world. With programmatic marketing and prediction machines, it's impossible to know what our intuition is telling us, except that 'something's fishy'.

Are we in tune with what we really need, what is essential? Do we know what's enough? As we advance as a species so too do our expectations–seemingly never quite met. We run the same old script of surplus, only now it's souped-up on steroids. And while this routine must surely be on its last legs, many relentlessly keep pumping. They don't know any other way. Subconsciously they have quashed any alternatives.

THE LOTTERY TICKET AND THE STRUGGLE

Writing about the Harvard M.B.A 'lottery ticket', Charles Duhigg, a graduate himself, explains that the degree has been a far cry from a gilded highway to meaningful work. Although wealthy and successful on the outside, many from his graduating class are professionally disappointed on the inside. Some are just plain miserable. As we've already seen, the dread of trudging into the office is a widespread phenomenon. Half the working world are dissatisfied in their jobs while many others are *actively* disengaged at work.

The payoff we're really seeking from work comes in the form of purpose, freedom, contribution, variation, validation, and challenge. It's why the smartest companies divvy people up into small dynamic units that promote good tribalism. 'We see these mission statements everywhere, mantras that are designed to inspire belonging and create unwavering loyalty to the company, but the biggest challenge particularly in big business is actually practicing what you preach,' declares devout shaper Edward Vince. Formerly at Facebook's in-house agency and now a Creative Director at Airbnb, Vince is surprised by how many organisations are simply out of touch with reality. This is precisely why there is a *Great Migration* to independent work–one that provides a better chance, or at least the hope of turning dreams into reality.

On the brighter side, overcoming setbacks may be part of the bittersweet journey. The virtues of the struggle create a righteous road towards meaning–in both work and life. 'The smoothest life paths sometimes fail to teach us about what really brings us satisfaction day-to-day,' writes Duhigg. Strangely, being in a precarious position provides the juicy opportunity to go after what you truly want. Quietening the *shoulds* and enveloping the *musts*, shapers step up to create working lives we love.

MINDSTATES AND PROFESSIONAL SUCCESS

Erica Avey liked her job. But after microdosing LSD for six months, she quit. Microdosing, for the unfamiliar, is taking a wee bit of psychedelics, typically acid or magic mushrooms. The tiny dose (roughly 1/10th of a normal trip) is said to help creativity, focus, and relationships as well as reduce the stresses of daily life. Besides altering the *tripper's* sense of time, however, the jury is still out on this one.

For Avey, she became all too aware that she wasn't doing anything meaningful at work. 'There was no more gray area of hanging around the office or poking around on Twitter, letting the time slip as the outside world turned. No more "should I stay or should I go" debacles in my head,' she recalls. Stagnation and stress were affecting her health and she could no longer turn a blind eye.

While making progress in work is a personal affair that doesn't mean dosing–a practice probably best reserved for the select few. What is required, however, is a healthy state of mind. Shapers need a coherent and compelling inner narrative that they are not spinning their wheels but indeed making headway. When we change the way we think, by whatever means, we alter not only how we feel but how we show up in the world. This *perspective-hacking* is really the rapid ability to change the way you look at things, whether it be through high-contrast conversations, journaling, meditation, travel, or some other practice. As George Clinton puts it: 'Free your mind, and your ass will follow.'

We know so little about the brain, and even less so about the mind. Researchers have discovered that autobiographical memory and mental time travel (reflecting on the past and rocketing ahead to the future) occur in our Default Mode Network (DMN). It's the conductor of our neural symphony and where our sense of self lives. When volunteer psilocybin trippers were placed in an fMRI machine, activity in the DMN reduced. In plain English, the ego disintegrates.

The DMN is also home to our theory of mind. It gives us the ability to understand and identify with the mental states of others. When we resonate with someone, it's in part because we can imagine what they're feeling. This plays out at work as we author our own stories while staying attuned to the stories of others. Doing this dance between independence and interdependence with more consciousness and grace leads to better approaches in how we work and live.

If microdosing isn't your bag (and even if it is), the more popular and perennial means to melt the ego is through meditation. As we touched on in Chapter 13, meditation is a sure-fire way to gain more clarity and equanimity. You reduce anxiety and stress while boosting focus and productivity. In lowering the activity in the DMN through meditation, in effect, you give the protagonist of your life story a well-deserved break.

With meditation you focus on *no-thing* and can become more mindful as a result. Being mindful then allows you to hone in on *some thing*; for example, seeing resentment build in your colleague for example. The big kerfuffle with mindfulness research in the workplace is that it can deflate people. Mindfulness doesn't affect work performance per se, but it sure as hell can lead to a loss in motivation. Employees may come to see the pointlessness of certain duties and question whether these can be outsourced, automated, or possibly dispensed with altogether. Others, in much the same way that Avey woke up, may come to realise that their office is just not a place they want to be in anymore.

The penultimate benefit of mindfulness is the ability to become more embodied–knowing how best to direct our energy. When organisations help people become more mindful workers, they kill two birds with one stone: promoting well-being as well as facilitating business innovation.

The penultimate benefit of mindfulness is the ability to become more embodied–knowing how best to direct our energy.

THE VIRTUES OF BOREDOM

While the virtues of boredom are long-standing within the arts, they can apply equally to knowledge work. Deliberate boredom–parading itself as active rest–is critical for problem solving and creative thinking. This listless time is strictly for recovery, not a sneak peek or prune of your socials. And if you're one of those people that works around-the-clock and thinks scheduling downtime is for pansies, think again. How we spend our time not working impacts how capable we are when we are working.

Planning a recess not only boosts creativity as your mind works through problems in the background, it also reduces your feeling of time pressure. And no, this does not need to be as drastic full-blown digital detox. Follow all that cognitively draining work you've done with deliberate rest. The creative benefits of walking, running, napping, loafing, meandering, playing, and generally mucking about (all in good measure) are now well known. The painter Marcel Duchamp was renowned for intentionally wasting time. Taking time out, then, can bring solace as well as make you more productive at work. If history is any indication, a bit of slacking really can be medicine for the soul.

Our daily lives are riddled with inputs–often if in the form of information overload. Shapers are extremely discerning with their inputs and look to make meaningful outputs. They slow down in order to speed up.

Research suggests that when you get busy (like real busy), your attention is hijacked. You simply can't take the time to control your time and exercise good judgement on how to best spend it. The net outcome, of course, is that you end up busy being busy *and* experiencing increased anxiety to boot. To refuel our minds, we need to relax on the regular. And while we may know the science-backed benefits of rest, most don't carve out nearly enough of this precious time.

> Shapers have woken up. They know that taking care of themselves means they can take care of business.

Taking time out to do nothing does take practice. 'It takes a lot of time to be a genius, you have to sit around so much doing nothing, really doing nothing' wrote author and poet Gertrude Stein. Dedicated times to bugger off have led to the discovery of many things we know and love: Scotch tape, sticky notes, and gravity to name but a few. Intuitively we know when we need to rest and yet it's easy to ignore this voice by powering through the day and pounding another latte.

We must be strong-willed to switch between focused work and the type of restorative breaks that permit serious navel-gazing. Shapers organise their day and their minds to ensure there is space for great ideas to happen. Another grand old way to recharge, if you can swing it, is by taking a sabbatical. Every six years famed designer Stefan Sagmeister religiously decamps for his. He shuts down his New York-based agency and is convinced that in doing so, he's investing in the long-term creative and commercial success of his firm.

Curbing the monkey mind, shapers train their brains through perspective-hacking to be right here, right now. This leads to better decision-making with a finer balance between objectivity and emotion. The irony, of course, is that our hunter-gatherer ancestors lived in this state. A heightened awareness of every sight, smell, touch, taste, and sound was essential for survival. Being too sensitive could mean death. My, how good we have it today as we fiddle over our meditation Apps.

'The gods were bored; therefore they created human beings', wrote Danish Philosopher Soren Kierkegaard. Relaxation is the key to our biggest breakthroughs–we have to find ways to be creative but also creative ways to relax. In the beeping and buzzing world in which we've found ourselves in, the trick is to be strategic in how we sprinkle restorative breaks into our busy schedules. Shapers make loafing non-negotiable so as to be unwavering in how they show up in the world.

Taking a timeout doesn't curb creativity, it catapults it. In a popular *New York Times* article on anxiety, author and cartoonist Tim Kreider wrote:

> Idleness is not just a vacation, an indulgence or a vice; it is as indispensable to the brain as vitamin D is to the body, and deprived of it, we suffer a mental affliction as disfiguring as rickets. The space and quiet that idleness provides

is a necessary condition for standing back from life and seeing it whole, for making unexpected connections and waiting for the wild summer lightning strikes of inspiration–it is, paradoxically, necessary to getting any work done.

The world is slowly remembering this.

So instead of opting to burn the midnight oil, we might make space to master the art of doing nothing much at all, drawing on that blissful state of boredom.

FINDING FLOW

At the height of the 1960s American counterculture, Robert Pirsig, along with his young son, set off on a trusty Honda Superhawk for the ride of a lifetime. The 17-day odyssey saw them crisscross the country from Minnesota to San Francisco, drunk on the expansive view of nature's gifts.

Pirsig would spend the next four years crafting *Zen and the Art of Motorcycle Maintenance*–a one-hit wonder that became the most read philosophy book of all time. It was his concoction of *working* and *not working* that would afford him extreme focus and originality. Pirsig was a connoisseur in the subtle art of doing nothing. 'Boredom on the job was an incentive to creativity. I deliberately enter a period of boredom just prior to writing … because ultimately it brings me down to the centre of things from which all creativity comes,' he explained in a rare 1974 interview.

Pirsig's views were a mash-up of Eastern and American philosophies, and paved the way for both Mihaly Csikszentmihalyi's notion of *Flow* and the Gladwellian ideas in *Outliers*. Pirsig called it Quality with a capital Q to show that breeding ground for creativity spawns a specific kind of event. The best moments of our lives often happen when we willingly stretch our minds to realise something that is both challenging and worthwhile. Or to put it more simply, we come alive when we feel the fullness of being.

Pirsig pursued the 'knife-edge' of experience so emphatically that he literally went mad. Perhaps because he was determined to dance a dangerous line, he fumbled upon enlightenment. Whichever way, seeing and living the truth, Pirsig became both immersed and paralysed in the present.

It's all fine and dandy to experience flow by losing yourself in your mind or in the forest–but how exactly does this flow translate to our work? It all comes down to whether we care–whether we feel a genuine connection to what we're working on: 'When one isn't dominated by feelings of separateness from what he's working on, then one can be said to "care" about what he's doing. That is what caring really is, a feeling of identification with what one's doing,' explained Pirsig while describing a skilled mechanic. This connection can manifest both in boredom and its flipside as flow. Shapers, of course, find it excruciating to do work they don't care about–so they do whatever it takes to change this.

SUSTAINING FLOW

Eminem was feeling the flow. It was the turn of the century when famed music producer Dr. Dre first laid eyes on the rapper who was sporting a blindingly bright yellow sweatsuit. Captivated, Dre invited the kid to record at his studio.

On one track, he blew Dre's wig back. Dropping 'Hi! My name is (what?)' impromptu over a sample, the song would become a Billboard Hot 100 and catapult Eminem's career. Sustaining flow is not reserved exclusively for music studios or sports arenas. The same psychological and physiological effects of flow-states can be realised in knowledge work.

When in flow you'll typically experience many things, but two things stick out like a sore thumb: 1) time feels suspended, and 2) the world and its demands melt away and you along with it.

This happens because the activity at hand is autotelic–it's done for its own sake. In many ways you're in a meditative state, albeit a moving one. Flow is really about these deep optimal experiences and being fully engaged in what we do.

The noise of the world quietens and we feel no pressure or concerns. Oh how lovely it is to be so intensely focused on the matter at hand that we lose ourselves in our work. A professional life full of this deepness can be a truly satisfying one.

While there's no conclusive evidence that flow leads to greater productivity in the workplace, there is strong evidence that our perceptions, emotions, and motivation over the course of the workday are improved. Even if we dupe ourselves into believing we *crushed it* in the morning, the residual effects can ride with us throughout the day. Especially for those activities that require both spontaneity and creativity, being in a positive mood can impact our performance. Just recall the lightness you feel when the wind is beneath your wings.

Nowhere are flow-chasing junkies more prevalent than in Silicon Valley. Engineers slurp soylent to avoid breaking their coding sprints while CEOs head off to Burning Man to orchestrate optimum experiences. They seek to make flow less erratic and stack their personal trickers to induce more flow experiences more frequently.

On the surface, the potency, duration, and regularity of flow experiences seem a worthy endeavour. Yet the optimal experience itself, when your body or mind is stretched to its absolute limits, isn't always joyful. It can mean putting yourself in extremely uncomfortable situations where willpower wavers, exhaustion ensues, and the rewards are not immediately reaped.

Shapers now have the opportunity to make work a more enjoyable expression, reflective of our strengths, character, and values. What we need is the right degree of challenge and skill so we can continually step into the zone. Company cultures also need to provide crystal clear goals and embed mechanisms to make sure we're not just doing O.K. but also perpetually challenged. The best way to do this as we've seen is to create a culture of trust and foster a safe space for employees to speak their mind as they gingerly step into the muck.

Understanding how we find our flow will be increasingly important as our work becomes more complex. Systematically getting into the groove takes practice. Shapers stay cognisant of when it's time to switch their surroundings. We are discerning about the specific type of work we're tackling. We stay attune to our mood.

We pay attention to our attention. And as we ourselves change and our work life is shaped in tandem, it's discipline that becomes our best mate.

THE ONGOING WOW

All too often we ignore those cues inside us so we can fit–or is it squeeze?–into a corporate setting. It's one thing to be unaware of an unhealthy work environment and another to knowingly stick it out day after day. We all have our own story, and there may very well be valid reasons for hanging around. But citing how it might be perceived on your LinkedIn is not one of them.

The career ladder has long since collapsed. We're now on a series of tours with dips and turns, bridges and freeways, exits ramps and roundabouts. Shapers cultivate flow, creating virtuous cycles that help fuel progress. Day after day, our positive feelings and interiority enable us to spiral up.

'The world of work that I entered in the 21st century looked very different to the world my parents entered in the 20th century, or my grandparents before them. I didn't embark on a one-career life like my Granddad, who was a veterinary surgeon for his whole professional career. I'm not going to progress in a linear fashion up the ladder of one organisation–assistant, manager, and executive.

My world of work, and how I work, looks very different,' writes Silvia Zuur, a director at PwC in New Zealand. The magic lies in discovering a colourful route, one full of splendour despite the unknown destination.

It's all a bit maddening to think that we can discover that *one thing* to contain the messiness and mystery of discovering oneself in work. College kids and high schoolers are expected to know what they want to do with the rest of their lives long before they know who they really are, let alone what they want. We're told to specialise. We're anxious about our competition. We scurry to stay relevant. Indeed, the fear of becoming dispensable is a big trigger for shame. And when the sense of making progress escapes us, we feel deflated.

For many, there's little point in desperately clinging to an old world of work when a new one has emerged. 'Seeing the collapse of the global financial system, having to start your career in a dire looking job market, and working for organisations that are exacerbating systemic social and environmental problems rather than solving them, have made many young people question the "business-as-usual" career. As a result, we have seen a wave of professionals choosing alternative career paths or transitioning from traditional employment into freelancing, entrepreneurship, part-time work, or leaving the system altogether,' explains Gen Zer Francesca Pick and longstanding member of the Enspiral Network.

As with love, we like to think that one career will not just endure, but fulfil us for a lifetime. Deep down we know this to be fantasy. 'Combining Romanticism and modern capitalism, as we are expected to do, is a near-impossible task,' claims philosopher Alain de Botton. In either arena of love or work, we hedge our bets on a single champion when there are several awaiting in the stable. There are so *many worlds* we could potentially live in.

Of course, you, just as I, could have been somebody else. There's no point agonising over it. When our actual self fails to measure up to our potential one,

> It's how we direct our energy, what we choose to do, that *shapes* who we become.

we seek distractions. We shop, gamble, game, gorge, binge, sext, and God knows what else just so long as it creates a diversion. Others give up, dropping out of society altogether.

America has an opioid crisis and a thirty-year high in suicide rates for a reason. 'There is always a gap between achievement and desire. Feeling like a failure is the inevitable price for harbouring any sort of ambition,' continues Botton. Giving life to an unexpressed self takes courage, but the possibility and the reward that awaits has never been riper. Because if not now, then when?

There's no time to waste, we can slay those stories that trap ourselves today. The promise of a bigger paycheck or promotion means little if deep down we know we're in shoes we don't wish to fill. At least from time to time, we all want and maybe need to feel the ongoing WOW happening right now.

While some cling to old ways of working, shapers see the Titanic sinking. We won't–heck we can't–suppress who we are for the sake of fitting in. Those who fail to speak up or do something about what's really going in their soul-destroying workplaces suffer devastating side-effects: resentment, infighting, poor mental health, physical ailments–the list goes on and on. Worse still, the emotionally toxic residue lingers–bringing it home at night and then lugging it back the next morning in a wicked loop. If this resonates in some way, then ask yourself what do you have control over? Recall the job crafting strategy from Chapter 7 and get crafty on figuring out how you can shift your stance, transform your work, and witness your colleagues change right in front of you.

Like it or not the future of work is emotional. With no masks to sport we can now let our badass selves glide into work. The benefits of being authentic outstrip the collateral damage of having to stuff away emotions and our human nature. This is, I think, the silver lining to the new way of working.

'We don't need to change our biology to be better at work, we need to change the way we work to be better for our biology,' affirms Avey. When your bullshit detector is sharp, the type of work environment that lifts you up becomes crystal clear. Eames chairs, well-stocked fridges, and daily yoga classes no longer cut it.

From our health and happiness to the cosmos and its creatures, we know there's too much at stake to pretend everything's hunky-dory. The world and the nature of work are changing, and the new way permits a deeper connection to ourselves and to others. Instead of crushing the soul, we can feed it. Shapers need to be bold in leading the way–because as more people watch us drink the Kool-Aid, they too will be gunning for a taste.

CHAPTER 16

LEADING: MODES OF SHOWING UP

New modes of leadership are premised on trust and the practice of management is now more art than science. The courageous leader is always asking 'How can I help my teams to do their best work?' with the emphasis being on function, not status. These shapers at the helm move easily between different modes of leading including the Teacher, Learner, Mobiliser, Giver, and Coach.

For the hellish efficiency Frederick Taylor created, karma came to bite him in the butt. Taylor, the oracle of time and motion studies, was stricken with insomnia, nightmares, and delirium. His scientific management turned out to be a charade and, more to the point, the practices are wholly unfit for the work we do today.

With the rise of knowledge work, a new model of management arose. McGill University professor Henry Mintztberg calls it 'emergent strategy'. In this model, every employee is given an opportunity to make certain decisions regarding their work and the organisation as a whole. Because power is dispersed throughout the organisation, each employee becomes a shaper–accountable for both revenue and culture. This resembles the self-management practices we explored in Chapter 11.

Modern management of an empowered workforce therefore requires an upgrade from an industrial mindset to one that is compatible with today's emergent era. We need different modes of leadership that are premised first and foremost on trust–more of an art than a 'science'. These modes include:

Leadership Mode	Description
➤ *Teacher*	➤ Providing clear direction, the requisite tools, and support—then getting out of the way

Leadership Mode	Description
➤ *Learner*	➤ Embracing change, encouraging experimentation, building courage, and learning from new ways of working
➤ *Mobiliser*	➤ Anticipating and responding to organisational needs and facilitating vital and timely change
➤ *Giver*	➤ Playing the long game by putting others first
➤ *Coach*	➤ Providing space and support to grow leaders who can think independently to solve their own problems and help others do so too

THE TEACHER

The business leader of tomorrow will not be seen as a boss. They will be more akin to a teacher that is in service of their employees. Their gift is to be a role model who makes their staff feel like students. They champion lifelong learning and feedback to advance individual growth and organisational progress.

The Teacher focuses on leading and educating by example. By distributing authority to team members, she champions transparency, knowledge sharing, continuous learning, and feedback. As cele-brated four-star general Stanley McChrystal puts it: the interplay between leaders and their teams is a case of 'eyes on, hands off.' In other words, the Teacher remains acutely aware of what her team is up to and how to best support them, but doesn't meddle for the sake of it.

In the tumultuous early years of Netflix, the company had to contract and expand its workforce due to a delayed IPO and the decline of DVDs and rising popularity of streaming. Under the wings of Patty Mccord, a culture was cultivated premised on *freedom* and *responsibility*. This included unlimited vacation days, the termination of formal performance reviews, and a radical expense policy (act in Netflix's best interests). Hiring 'brilliant jerks' of course was avoided at all costs. And every leader was crystal clear on her most important task: to build great teams. Netflix bucked the norm, you guessed it, by treating people like adults.

The leader as Teacher looks to a unique set of results. They are measuring *return on trust*. They do not tolerate complacency or backstabbing and help steer norms that lead to a conscientious and courageous culture. When workers can reciprocally treat each other as competent professionals, they become accountable, empowered, and engaged. Leaders who get this are simply setting the stage: agreeing on a clear direction, providing workers with what they need to get there, and then getting the hell out of their way.

THE LEARNER

As industrial systems grow ever larger and more complex, leaders must quickly develop the expertise to assemble the right resources, at the right time, from the right departments.

The leader as Learner requires an intellectually curious mind. With this disposition she can sway the entire dynamic of the organisation, helping to make teams more flexible and risk friendly. At times, they can be vulnerable. When these types of leaders admit they don't have all the answers (or even the right questions!) they then work closely with their teams to develop solutions.

Microsoft CEO Satya Nadella embodies the leader-as-learner style. His fervent advocacy to adopt a *beginner's mind* has had a profound impact on the company's culture, innovation capabilities, and commercial success. He has completely turned the ship around by ridding it of the former 'know-it-all' attitude and supplanting it with a 'learn-it-all' philosophy. And this is all from a humble engineer who spends his leisure time reading poetry and taking online neuroscience classes.

In the army's Ranger Regiment there is an organisational relationship predicated on age-old promises. Belief in one another runs deep. In a similar vein, the bond between employees enabled through enlightened leadership, McChrystal explains, is one where: 'Leaders can let you fail, yet not let you be a failure.'

Learners are conduits, synthesising and applying information–providing a key intersection along information paths. They are self-cultivators who continually rise up. They possess the wherewithal to take meaningful action based on their learning. This catalytic learning ability first requires searching for new ideas, then integrating them, and finally using them to advance the organisation.

Leaders as learners establish a learning organisation by making experimentation a virtue. Failing is only taboo if you fail to learn from it.

THE MOBILISER

The Mobiliser is acutely aware of organisational needs. As new information emerges from different and sometimes far-flung teams, it's the Mobiliser who responds with enlightened choices, bringing others into the fold to prompt collective action from the team.

As a fresh-eyed CEO of industrial conglomerate Alcoa, Paul O'Neill spent much of his time listening. He decided to put all his chips on the table and focus on one thing: safety. He encouraged every employee to share information about worker safety. They did, and gradually started sharing all sorts of other information–including ways to boost efficiency and productivity.

Focusing on one item caused a domino effect across the organisation. Alcoa became one of the first companies to use an intranet, catapulting it light years ahead of its competitors. O'Neill's safety culture completely transformed the business; Alcoa witnessed a 5x increase in net income and $27 billion in market capitalisation.

THE GIVER

Soft-spoken, selfless, a big collaborator, and an all-around nice guy–these are not the characteristics you'd typically expect of someone at the helm of one of the world's largest companies. Yet that's exactly what Sundar Pichai is known for as the CEO of Google. His management style is pretty darn simple: helping others succeed. Pichai typifies the Giver who thrives in the new economy.

Abraham Lincoln was a Giver. He set ego aside, appointing his bitter opponents to the Cabinet knowing this would best serve the entire country. Lincoln was known for putting the interest of others before his own. Adam Grant, who we encountered in Chapter 6, explains that in stark contrast to Takers, when Givers succeed, something extraordinary happens: '[Success] spreads and cascades.'

Not surprisingly, companies that foster a culture of giving report more profitability, productivity, efficiency, and customer satisfaction. And when a leader has Giver qualities, it also helps to attract top talent and lower turnover rates. So while Takers might win the 100-metre sprint, Givers win gold in marathons.

THE COACH

When Meghan Messenger joined the e-commerce marketplace *Next Jump*, it was as an intern. Over the next two decades she would rise through the ranks to become co-CEO. She helped create one of the world's foremost *deliberately developmental organisations* (DDO). A DDO is an incubator for personal and professional development. It fosters collective responsibility to achieve a learning environment that is continuously adapting. In short, it supports and elevates you to be a badass.

Next Jump's big leap took place after the dot-com bust in the early 2000s. They had dwindled from 150 to 4 employees and were back at the drawing board. This time around they would take a radically different approach–making all new hires accountable for both revenue and culture. By virtue, every worker could grow to become a leader.

Messenger became a great leader only by letting go of the reins. Indeed, her style of leadership–honest, expressive, and emotional–embodies the feminine spirit. In a world that has become increasingly interdependent, feminine values lay the foundation for our 21st-century operating system. The proof is in the pudding: Next Jump has over 200 people thriving as leaders in the organisation.

Messenger exemplifies coaching as a leadership capability. Through her courage and encouragement, she models behaviour and inspires others to follow suit. She disperses power throughout the organisation and creates space for people to rise to be their best. The impact at the individual and institutional level is profound–better morale, engagement, creativity, and productivity. And what of financial performance? In 2016, revenue spiked significantly exceeding $2 billion dollars. Next Jump is the paragon of an inclusive culture where everyone is supported and elevated to be their best selves.

The leader as coach sees the potential in others. They let people shape their own work because they know they're naturally creative, resourceful and whole. Using their own smarts to boost the intelligence of others they can make geniuses. This type of leader doesn't tell people what to do; instead they offer up suggestions on ways to better navigate work. Operating on the assumption that people are doing their best, the leader as coach provides a framework for workers to be even better. Success is not an individual affair but achieved through deliberately designing, motivating, supporting, and elevating high performing teams.

WHAT EVERY LEADER SHOULD BE ASKING

All five models focus on building transparency by being radically candid. Which one to use at any given time begins with the question: how can I help my teams do their best work? Leaders that get this are not just making the workplace more human, they're also fostering better financial performance. The two are not mutually exclusive. Companies with high degrees of trust surpass the average annualised returns of S&P 500 businesses by a factor of three.

Mintzberg's model leader, according to his colleague Karl Moore, sees that, 'Strategy emerges over time as intentions collide with and accommodate a changing reality.' This adaptive way of leading can't be neatly stored inside a pre-ordained plan, for the simple fact that it must bubble up from within the business. This is precisely why we need emergent leadership–the kind where a designated leader is more than happy to let someone else drive so long as he or she gets a seat on the bus.

BYE BYE BOSS

Leaders can't help fix problems that they don't know about. It's their employees on the front line who are closest to organisational challenges that can. With an integrated approach founded upon complete transparency and knowledge sharing, efficacious leaders cook resiliency into their teams. Employees become shapers who are accountable, empowered, and engaged.

Nine out of every ten managers don't have what it takes to be great. Tackling this reality head-on means progressive training and development, or where applicable, getting rid of managers all together. Employee disengagement can be flipped on its head to become employee empowerment. 'Control leads to compliance, autonomy leads to engagement,' as Daniel Pink puts it.

What will great leadership look like in the future? Actively distributing authority to enable individuals and teams to make quicker and smarter decisions. It will entail operating from a place of what one can *learn*, not from what one *knows*.

The shaper in a leadership role appreciates the intricacies of teams, how to harness talent, and inspire loyalty. They empower their colleagues by instilling open ways of working. Regretfully, we just don't have many role models for these more enabling leadership practices. 'So not only are people not learning this approach in their professional training, they're not seeing it in action in their organisations. Instead, they're often seeing the same old approach–and worse, they're often seeing this approach rewarded with promotions,' explains Pink.

Bold leaders prioritise transparency, empathy, creativity, and being of service. They develop a repository of skills and tools to quickly and effectively deal with ambiguity. The *dirty yes* (saying yes to your face and no behind your back) and *shadow talking* (moaning to others about you or something that you did rather than saying it to your face) are not tolerated. As organisational designers, they create psychologically safe environments for teams to be as fluid and effective as possible. People are then comfortable saying what they mean and are committed to doing what they say.

The same norms that you would uphold with those closest to you are present in working teams–so nobody 'gets dressed' to go to work. Vulnerability, experimentation, and learning through failure are rewarded, not avoided. A bias towards action and a propensity for rapid and ongoing experimentation are essential. Micromanaging is avoided and an inclination towards action and a propensity for ongoing experimentation is encouraged. What's valued is productive work rather than time recorded on the clock.

In this *new school,* continuous learning is compulsory. The shaper as leader embodies a growth mindset that others emulate. Through regular, honest, and reciprocal feedback everyone continuously improves. Skills development is encouraged. Teamwork is inspired. And developing a personal toolkit for life is par for the course.

These new modes of leadership are much more suited to the networked world we live in. Here, leaders learn to wear different hats at different times. They perform an intricate dance between teaching, learning, giving, mobilising, and coaching. They enable workers to bring their entire selves to the office and not just their professional selves. This is what cultivates a motivated, empowered, and engaged squad of shapers. Winning becomes a team sport–shared and celebrated throughout the organisation.

CHAPTER 17

BECOMING: OUR SOCIAL FABRIC

Our anxiety is not just an individual pathology but a collective one. With intention directed to the right things, we can gain a semblance of sanity amid increasing uncertainty. Social intelligence and the cunning ability to connect with, and relate well to others will be essential to thrive in the future. Those who choose to shape more colourful working lives for themselves will in turn make the system of work, and the world, more humane.

We're irrational, fallible, and complicated beings. Our beauty rests in our imperfection. And so it goes with our organisations that we build in our image. The challenge, and the opportunity, is to understand this truth.

Shapers see work not as something to get right but as an emergent practice. We approach work with a different weight. We are lighter. The aim isn't so much praise (although it's nice to be appreciated from time to time), as it is to adapt and continuously improve.

And when we see our organisations for what they are–complex adaptive systems–we can tend to them like gardens. Shapers appreciate the variety of interacting components and predict how they will change over time and in different environments. As such we facilitate, rather than inhibit, their mutation.

Our idiosyncrasies–whether they manifest through the stressors of work today or the anxiety about tomorrow–shouldn't be banned from the office. Feelings don't remained snuggled up home when we head off to work. Last I heard, people will always be people.

The culture at IDEO encourages people to be themselves and come up with zany projects and quirky events. One designer created a digital GIF machine and installed it on the office walls. Employees walked up and filmed themselves dancing or doing whatever and it then automatically sent them the GIF. If that doesn't put a smile on a face, I don't know what will.

Now while that degree of zaniness may be a bit far-fetched for many organisations, the point is not missed: even if just for a moment, giving people space to be themselves allows them to feel human. Sure, having this liberty creates its own set of challenges. Some employees may not cope as well as others in these authentic work environments. Others may come to discover their true calling and simply up and leave. Still others may be exposed doing the bare minimum and will need to either get their act together quick or face getting fired.

The benefits of fostering safe workspaces where you can be your badass self outweigh the drawbacks. Feeling human at work is essential for morale, connection, inspiration, and creativity. We've seen that with a clear sense of purpose, the requisite agency, and ongoing support, people flourish. Our systems of work should reflect our values and uphold our humanity. We're often far more resourceful than others give us credit for, it's just that we're not provided the opportunity to shine.

When we spend one third of our lives at work, isn't it rather silly to ignore the truths of who we are? To dismiss our nature and stuff our true selves inside a cubby? Might we do better to address what's really going on–to say what we really mean–instead of dropping clues to our colleagues so they can play Sherlock Holmes? This is not to imply that our colleagues need to double up as shrinks; it simply means that we don't have to pretend to be someone we're not. We can reveal ourselves to others as well as to ourselves.

WE CONTAIN MULTITUDES

The Advanced Research Project Agency Network (ARPANET), the building block for the Internet, was well underway in the late 1960s. The previous two decades had been marked by prosperity, rising wages, and advertising. At the time, sociologist Alvin W. Gouldner wrote a scathing essay demonstrating how organisations employ only the parts of people that are useful to them, discarding the rest. 'The world of work then is one of human insufficiency or of downright failure in the midst of technological triumph, of personal confusion in the midst of detailed organisational blueprints,' he wrote.

If we deem a work activity to be void of utility, it's typically shaved from our professional identity. Sometimes we suppress parts of our professional selves out of fear, habit, laziness, or an impulse to conform. Over a lifetime, several parts of ourselves will lay dormant and a plethora of paths forever unexplored. With the pressures to specialise, the desire to belong, and in the service of capitalism–it's just the way it's been. We've become numb to the multitude of potential selves that we alienate. But the 'unemployed self' still yearns for a chance to stretch its legs.

As the world shifts and the Internet enters middle age, it's not a terrible time to reflect and reassess. 'The system rewards and fosters those skills deemed useful and suppresses the expression of talents and faculties deemed useless, and thereby structures and imprints itself upon the individual personality and self,' continues Goulnder. If we play this out, we'll continue, rather masochistically, to punish ourselves for failing to conform to a dysfunctional system.

The digital network and rapid technological progress only amplify our malaise–only deepen an anti-human agenda. Full-time professionals march into the office each day leaving more and more of themselves at home. And we uphold the status quo of divorcing the whole person from work. This inability for honest expression tears at our sense of self and fluffs our clouds of doubt. And through this collective neurosis, we'll short-circuit.

What we desperately need now is not a better software framework, but an entirely new hardware replacement. *Slashies,* those who pursue multiple career paths simultaneously, are doing the next best thing: hacking the system. Think of the UX Designer/Disc Jockey/Yoga Instructor who is frowned upon by some and envied by others. Walk into an Ace Hotel Lobby in London or New York and you'll be hard-pressed to find someone who isn't a *slashie.* Maintaining this portfolio of work is a sensible way to avoid the current alternatives that squander the human spirit. It satiates, although fleetingly at times, the craving for variety.

Of course, the *slashie* life is not foolproof. Many would find it overwhelming, exhausting, and way too precarious for their liking. This way of working may be a strategy to hedge bets on a range of careers or a temporary band-aid until a more appealing gig comes along. It's also a rather righteous path to setting up a proper shop. Unrestricted by selling time–and generating ongoing revenue through smart systems that 'scale themselves'–*slashies* mature into companies of one, in effect becoming shapers. 'It turns out that the most successful brand name companies and individuals are companies of one at heart,' writes author Paul Jarvis. Whichever way it manifests, it feels good to humour a range of inclinations and not betray the inner callings of the self.

If the workplace doesn't let us be ourselves, we have choices: change the culture, change ourselves, or up and leave. We may not have control over external events, but we can control our responses to them. Indeed, a sense of belonging and fulfillment will only arise if we project it onto our work and those environments in which we operate. We can refuse to spend our days in an elaborate exercise of posturing and fake productivity and instead choose to continually learn, experiment more, and cooperate better. No doubt, *becoming is better than being.*

When we are curious and courageous enough to move beyond our self-perceived limits, we find that more possibilities open up to us. We affect those around us through our creativity and resilience. When we renew ourselves and what we value in work, it provides the opportunity to repair the estrangement we have with our 'unemployed selves'. Ask yourself which parts of you lay dormant and should finally be laid to rest? And which parts are chomping at the bit to be given life to?

We can retrieve those parts of us, and values they bring, that are in jeopardy of being lost. These are the very idiosyncrasies that make us human. More of our passions, capacities, skills, and gifts can be set free. If we won't let it, the human spirit needn't feel cramped any longer.

RACING WITH THE MACHINES

Those machines, dang them. If we perfect the marriage between humanity and technology we'll arrive at our final destination. We will think better and run faster. We will work less and play more. With the aid of our mechanical minds, we can tweak our personal settings and overnight become an impressionist painter, tennis star, polyglot, or day trader. Heck, why not have it all while we're at it? Let's be sure to upload our brains to the web for safe-keeping. And what of death? No worries mate, we got your back–we're solving that one too. This is the transhumanist agenda at full tilt.

This kind of thinking is: 'What you get when people who have read Dawkins would still rather like there to be a rapture. It's a fundamentally Christian without knowing it, hilariously patriarchal, profoundly politically dubious movement made entirely of fantasists too cowardly to deal with the realities of the entirety of human biology and too narrow-minded to understand either the nature of consciousness or their place in the world … and they're all dudes, for one thing. It's worth asking why,' comments technologist Ben Hammersley.

Transhumanism is valuable not for the promise of living forever, but for revealing what it means to be human when we don't exist eternally. As they were massacred, Native Americans believed that Europeans colonists surely were possessed by evil spirits. *Wettiko,* as Native Americans called it, was the colonists' delusional belief that stealing the life force of others was a logical and moral behaviour. Likewise, directing our hearts and minds towards a post-human future is itself a disease. We're performing *cyber-wettiko* explains media theorist Douglass Rushkoff–only this time it's on all of us.

We're trapped on an optimisation hamster wheel. Any friction in our lives is to be identified and then removed. Every problem can be solved. Every desire fulfilled. And on it goes. The dilemma is that: 'The transhumanist movement is less a theory about the advancement of humanity than a simple evacuation plan ... but their ideas just extend our same blind addiction to consumption, destruction, progress, and colonisation,' writes Rushkoff.

Instead of racing against the machines, we might consider a brisk walk alongside each other. Like it or not, we are enmeshed with technology. Automation (that fuels the transhumanism dialogue) is nothing new. When the Excel spreadsheet came along, millions of accountants had to stop using their eraser and start using their minds. Accountancy is shaped by Excel, you'd be hard pressed to get work as an accountant without employing it.

We hear the same old story of how machines will eat our jobs, yet new ones will be created. What we don't hear about as often is how many of these displaced workers will not be able to move into different new roles. While 19th century wagon drivers became cabbies, many will not be so lucky and face a much gloomier fate: that of the superfluous horse.

Many won't be exploited but will become something much worse: irrelevant. It's one reason why academics, entrepreneurs, and parents alike struggle to understand what people should study today. The answer might be not to learn for the sake of getting a job, but for the value of becoming a better person.

One of the main oversights about machines taking over work, and the world for that matter, is our misunderstanding of intelligence. Other animals can swim or fly across continents. But we have cleverer brains. It's conceivable that we build brains that surpass our human ones. However, this implies that we're thinking of intelligence in terms of a single dimension. From the logical to the linguistic, the emotional to the intellectual, and beyond–we know there are a host of intelligences. As of 2009, developmental psychologist Howard Gardner offered another one (existential intelligence) to his famous eight. Intelligence itself is not linear but something beautifully expansive.

Ambiguity, quirkiness, and suffering can't be codified. We're cognitively diverse and, at times, ridiculous. 'Conscious' robots that can experience love and loss? Well that just makes for a great Netflix special.

The geniuses of tomorrow should not be super-intelligent machines that have come to reign in the Singularity. But they could be super-teams comprised of human and mechanical minds. 'Whatever futurists may speculate about the singularity, right now and for the foreseeable future it is human beings, not algorithms, who will decide whether technology will make our lives better or worse,' writes Matthew Taylor of the Royal Society for the Encouragement of the Arts, Manufactures, and Commerce.

The aim then is not to fuse our brains with silicon ones, but to design for the intricate dance between the two. We already see this coupling escalating in the knowledge economy, transportation sector, and manufacturing industries. Robot surgeons are transforming healthcare and autonomous weapon systems are no longer the realm of science fiction.

Should our ethics corrode and we lose our way, the future will certainly be bleak. It's one thing to have delusions of grandeur believing you're better than others, but an entirely different matter when you believe you're superhuman and you actually are. Technology will always be a double-edged sword, the choice rests with us in how it's applied.

The machines, and the companies that run them, value us for our data which we gleefully fork over. These smart algorithms then chomp away so as to predict (and in many cases influence) our behaviour. They stain our social fabric. While technology may well be running in the background, it doesn't have to run us.

If we reframe our relationship with machines so that they're optimised for us (and not the other way around), we may find ourselves with the greatest opportunity to flourish. We can then set course on celebrating our humanity in all its grime and glimmer.

Cultural anthropologist Margaret Mead would surely be egging on team human if she were alive. 'If we are to achieve a richer culture, rich in contrasting values, we must recognize the whole gamut of human potentialities, and so weave a less arbitrary social fabric, one in which each diverse human gift will find a fitting place.' Try sticking this in a computer and see how it 'solves' for humanity. We're mysterious for a reason and we're wired not to be caged, but to be connected.

SAME OLD SONG AND DANCE

Somehow, I ended up at a gaudy launch event south of Market Street in San Francisco. Legendary soul singer James Brown was the guest of honour. I envisioned seeing him in a different setting–one full of sweaty dancers, kooks, and funksters, but this would have to make do. Never have I witnessed the level of glitz and glam. It was the turn of the century and was a time of excess–extravagance was expected.

The host, a music startup, was rumoured to take your compact discs purchased in-store and 'immediately' convert them to digital. Whoo hoo! Needless to say, that business is not around today. Like so many other technological disruptions, the MP3 changed the way we experience music forever.

The information revolution, with the advance of the microchip and the web, saw a frenzy of activity until the early 2000s. Y2K had been a sham. And with the dot-com boom and bust and later The Great Recession, entrepreneurs, investors, and the general public tread differently. They could decipher the signal from the noise. But this cycle is nothing new. Famed scholar Carlota Perez has demonstrated this pattern of paradigm shifts. And as you read this, we may very well be in the fifth great surge of development in the past 250 years.

Cycles of innovation are a funny thing. In the beginning we're like kids in a candy store in the beginning. Only after gorging on Snickers bars do we inevitably crash. As mature adults we still eat sweets, only in a more practical fashion. It takes longer, about fifty years to be more precise, for a new technology to mature. Reckless at the start, a new innovation must first be *installed* with a sound supportive infrastructure. And only when it has 'grown-up' can it be effectively deployed to the masses.

'Each technological revolution brings with it, not only a full revamping of the productive structure, but eventually a transformation of the institutions of governance, of society, and even of ideology and culture,' Perez writes. Depending on where you live, and what colour spectacles you look through, we may very well be in, or entering a golden age. Tomorrow's history books will decide.

But *this time* it's different! That's what they keep saying (I wonder who precisely *they* are? Would absolutely love to sit down for a chat). It is hard to argue against the massive technological progress we've made in the past decades. We now hold the same computing power in one hand as NASA scientists stored in all their entire control room during the Apollo mission. But the point is that the patterns that mark such drastic change tend to remain the same. It is our shifting values and evolving culture that distinguish between progress and oppression, between ignorance and enlightenment. We determine if the pattern will be disrupted and if the fabric of human history will be ruptured.

The historical record: Bubble prosperities, recessions and golden ages

Source: Perez, C. (2016) 'Capitalism, technology and a green global golden age: The role of history in helping to shape the future', in Jacobs, M. and Mazzucato, M. (eds) *Rethinking Capitalism: Economics and Policy for Sustainable and Inclusive Growth*. Chichester, West Sussex, United Kingdom: Wiley-Blackwell, p. 195.

Some of the greatest thinkers of the past were confident that science, technology, and human cooperation would mark the end of labour and set humanity free once and for all. They were living in a time when most work was absolutely dreadful. The Religious–Industrial Complex has since been abandoned, and the search for meaning happens through work. Work has evolved into a deliberate and spiritual practice of sorts–where creativity, expression, and contribution are the name of the game.

This is our watershed moment, but it's not about reaching full automation. It's about the view we take, and setting our sights towards a horizon where more humans reach their full potential.

CHAPTER 18
FUTURING: THE LONG VIEW

The crisis of work is not a problem to solve; it's a grand narrative to rewrite. We ditch our current short-term thinking to take the long view. We redefine our values and stretch the very meaning of work. We start to repair the world by ensuring that the dignity and opportunities that come with having a good livelihood spread to as many people as possible. And we realise this through a connected story of the contribution we each can make.

Compared to 200 years ago, we live like kings. We've nearly eradicated extreme poverty and a host of life-threatening diseases. Chimneys, toilets, dishwashers, and laundry machines have transformed life for the better, as have telecommunications, computers, and the Internet. We have modern agriculture, healthcare, education, and transportation. It's a fantastic time to be alive… especially if you're rich and in charge.

In just the past four decades, the US economy has more than tripled from $6.31 trillion dollars to $19.02 trillion. But in about the same period, while America was becoming more productive, real hourly wages stagnated and in some cases fell. The ratio of pay between the average worker and his or her boss skyrocketed from 22:1 to 271:1. The middle class hollowed out and shrunk by a whopping 60%. These same trends can be seen in other developing nations, with African and Latin American countries measuring the most unequal in the world.

While resources are abundant for nearly half the world, for the other half, these same resources are scarce. The 26 richest billionaires own the same value of assets as the 3.8 billion poorest people. This is our new gilded age.

Leading economist Mariana Mazzucato explains that the social, economic, and political impacts of this wealth division are devastating. Social mobility, access to good education, equal opportunities, and job security have become pipe dreams for all too many. People are working harder than ever and still, the modern economy leaves them behind. And when elites rule society, as Plato explains in *The Republic*, '[S]uch a city should of necessity be not one, but two, a city of the rich and a city of the poor, dwelling together, and always plotting against one another.'

We've confused value extraction with value creation. And this adversely affects companies, workers, society, and our planet. Reflecting on the ugliest truth facing America, growing economic inequality is a glaring signal to the misery that lies ahead. It is time to renew the values we value most.

PRODUCTIVITY PUZZLE

It would appear that the productivity miracle underlying the Americanised way of life was a one-time deal. When land, labour, and capital yield more than in the past, Total Factor Productivity (TFP) is said to be on the up. TFP measures leftover productivity gains after accounting for the growth of the workforce and capital investments. TFP has gone flat, as have overall living standards. Economists continue to scratch their heads in bewilderment at what's become known as the 'productivity puzzle.'

To put it more alarmingly: 'We're poorer, working longer hours, and leaving a worse world for our grandchildren than we otherwise would be,' explains journalist Ezra Klein. Life expectancy in the US is declining, yet American hospitals are the best in the world. Startups operate in a winner-take-all economy where a meager few must capture the bulk of the growth in a ballooning economy. Today, a sound business strategy is to sex yourself up so one of a handful of platform monopolies devours you.

To add more fuel to the fire, we face acute employee disengagement, a shortage of skilled labour, widespread inequality, underemployment, and machines that continue to gobble up our jobs. Oh yes, and millennials are having to endure the bleakest financial future of any generation in over a century.

While the amount of stuff the US makes continues to explode, American manufacturing employment has plummeted. 'The whole idea that [America] is moving towards lower employment is a myth. We've faked lower employment through extremely extractive, exploitative, polluting, and unsustainable business practices,' contends Douglas Rushkoff. Typically, the jobs that low-skilled workers enter are highly precarious and the work can be unkind to both humans and the planet.

We shouldn't forget that what we consume governs what we produce, and this then determines the nature of the jobs we have on offer. The subtext is that while our business practices compress labour so that fewer people can make more things, we externalise a myriad of other problems at the same time. It's clear that the industrial age imperative for efficiency and the subsequent ways we organise, grow, and compete no longer serve us. We're spinning our wheels in what can best be described as a turbo-charged hedonic Peloton stationary bike.

We continue to work harder without getting ahead and we suffer from a ubiquitous low-grade malaise littered with bouts of loneliness and existential dread. And, says the author of *How to do Nothing*, Jenny Odell, 'the attention economy has a financial incentive to keep us in a state of individualised anxiety and an obligation to constantly be reacting and producing.' Efficiency and resiliency have always been in tension with one another–and now more than ever–we need the collective psychological strength to adapt in the face of adversity.

Might we be going about measuring productivity ass-backward? We could include a metric of wellbeing in the index to gauge how well we're performing. We could follow New Zealand's lead and, instead of designing budgets strictly under an economic umbrella, recognise the impact on natural, social, human, and cultural capital. We might also appreciate how technology has helped us save time, connect us on a colossal scale, educate us in novel ways, and endlessly entertain us. Indeed, we've become more productive as humans and consumers, but not necessarily as workers.

THE FUTURE OF LESS WORK

Our planet is literally burning up. Small wonder the Oxford Dictionary's word of 2019 was 'climate emergency.' In June 2019, a southern province in Iraq clocked an 'ungodly' 55.6 degrees Celsius (132.08 degrees Fahrenheit). The following month marked the hottest month ever recorded on our pale blue dot.

Some leading climate experts warn that we're approaching a point of no return, a path where just a slight jump in temperature spells catastrophe: droughts, floods, extreme heat, and poverty for hundreds of millions. If we don't push the climate emergency to the top of the global agenda, there won't be *any* future, let alone work to do.

One factor that will help is shortening the workweek. Not only can this reduce our carbon footprint, it may also provide more opportunity to engage in our communities as conscientious workers, citizens, and neighbours.

Paul Lafargue, the son-in-law of Karl Marx, proposed a three-hour workday and the 'necessity to be lazy' as far back as the late 1800s. Economist John Maynard Keynes proposed the 15-hour workweek in the 1930s and predicted that it would take effect by 2030 (there's still a fighting chance, albeit a slim one). Around the same time, philosopher Bertrand Russell advocated for the four-hour workday in an essay for *Harper's Magazine*. And in 1984, management guru Charles Handy envisioned the rise of the output-driven portfolio worker and the accompanying freedom to work smarter, not longer. We've been slow to get the memo that all of these pioneering thinkers have sent us.

The DREAM for *working less* is convincing:

> ➤ **Dutifulness:** commute to offices less often so as to decrease greenhouse gas emissions, improve productivity, boost civic engagement, and enhance wellbeing.
>
> ➤ **Richness:** expand our leisure with time prosperity, living life well with family and friends, and enjoyable hobbies and other activities.
>
> ➤ **Enoughness:** slash material consumption and reduce our toxic economic behaviour.
>
> ➤ **Adeptness:** it's not jobs we need but quality work.
>
> ➤ **Mindfulness:** see beyond wage work and make time for things like cleaning, dog-walking, caretaking, and other activities so often outsourced.

'Work a short time, rest well and learn a lot,' is what Microsoft Japan president and CEO Takuya Hirano recalled of their four-day workweek trial. In late 2019, Microsoft completed the Work-Life Choice Challenge, which saw 2,300 workers take five Fridays off in a row without a pay cut. Productivity soared forty percent.

But what also occurred is more nuanced: happier workers, more efficient meetings, reduced levels of fatigue, and an overall improvement in health.

The benefits of working less also mean fewer sick days, cost savings, and a better work/life balance. With an improved sense of well-being and self-respect, workers tend to be more creative, committed, and collaborative. Autonomy, a UK-based Future of Work think tank, reports that a shorter workweek, amongst many benefits, also increases gender equality. On the flipside, when we work overtime, it causes stress, anxiety, and sometimes depression. It can also lead to more injuries and chronic illnesses in the short and long term.

The sweet spot for a working week is twenty-five to thirty hours. Scientific research has shown that the limit of our cognition is four-and-a-half hours of deep attention work per day, after which point we're kaput. Our productivity wanes when we overwork, with some reports claiming that working over twenty-five hours per week makes you more stupid–especially for those over the age of 40.

The Danes got it right; they work short hours and still have a flourishing economy. In Finland, teachers work some of the shortest workdays in the nation, allowing them to stay refreshed and engaged–a key contributor that makes their educational system one of the best in the world. At the time of writing, Finnish Prime Minister Sanna Marin has called for the entire country to move to a four-day workweek. Meanwhile, the stress and burnout caused by overworking costs the UK economy billions every year.

A shorter workweek means companies can reduce costs for items such as energy, electricity, food, commuting allowances, and variable office perks. Some firms might reduce salaries for a shorter workweek and use the extra cash for long-term investments in their people, to improve their education, talent and skills. And less work for some could actually mean freeing up more good work for others.

Shapers know that the secret to working smarter and not harder comes down to managing your energy. It means paying attention to your attention, not letting others rule your day, batching your work, and doing one task at a time.

The hoopla surrounding working less is about giving more control to workers over how they work to yield better outcomes. It's trading in the bulky industrial overcoat for a luminous information cape. If I can finish my daily tasks in five hours why should I remain on the job and fake being productive for the remaining three? If we get our act together, these changes could mean a new age of fulfilling work and a better way of life.

We should be wary though of how a company's workplace strategy may sell the sizzle but not the steak. Corporations could weaponise the shorter workweek. 'There are many examples of working practices that suit capital far more than they suit workers and yet have been sold as increasing freedom or improving the nature of the work itself,' insists technologist Ben Hammersley. The open office plan is a classic case in point. The concept itself was intended to give workers more freedom, but instead, it robbed them of essential private space. That nasty habit of lunching at one's desk is really a direct result of a design intervention gone sour.

Corporations could also tout a shorter working week as a PR stunt while expecting workers to work longer days. Employees may feel implicit pressure to work on days off or over weekends. Of course, all these companies will be missing the whole point of working less: to boost efficiency and become outcomes driven. Those workers who fake productivity and try to escape by just doing the bare minimum will stick out like a sore thumb. They'll need to shape up or ship out.

'I believe that in this century, we can win a four-day working week, with decent pay for everyone,' asserts Frances O'Grady, the head of the Trades Union Congress in England. Brits believe it too–61% of UK workers think a four-day working week would make them more productive. In short, productivity gains would be shared broadly to allow for radically shorter working hours and thus a qualitatively fairer society.

A WORLD BEYOND WAGES

There's an Albanian saying that translates loosely as: 'Those who work eat. Those who don't work, eat and drink.' Having too much free time will surely lead to wickedness, so the logic goes. Yet trial after trial of Universal Basic Income (UBI) initiatives shows that this is far from the truth.

UBI is all too often misunderstood. For starters, there is little agreement on what *universal* and *basic* entail. All trials have been at a national level so, although the notion of a universally distributed income is interesting, in practice it's each country deciding what's right for its citizens. As for basic, it's subjective. What's deemed essential to inhabitants of Norway may be viewed as luxuries to those in Namibia.

Secondly, UBI suffers from a terrible branding campaign. It's disquieting for many because it feels like a handout to slackers and an official funeral for 'working hard and getting ahead.' But this assessment misses the mark. We can think of basic income as the 'ration card that gives you access to all that is scarce in the world,' as Peter Frase writes in *Four Futures*.

In its purest form UBI is non-discriminatory. Instead of inequitable, convoluted, and fragmented welfare programmes, it's plain and simple, free money.

At a psychological level, UBI is a social experiment to see what happens when every citizen receives the same benefit, regardless of how much they earn. And at a systems level, it's anticipating a future that is hospitable to those who are pushed out of paid work. If ever there was a time for this to be taken to heart, it's now.

UBI schemes could also give workers an out if their boss is a scumbag, says writer Tom Streithorst. 'With UBI,' he notes, 'you can tell your boss to "take this job and shove it." It is like a strike fund for everyone.' By the same token, Streithorst acknowledges, 'The danger of UBI is that we will turn into those people in *Wall-E*, sitting on barcaloungers, stuffing our faces and watching TV. My hope is that we will follow our dreams instead of being stuck in dead-end jobs that rot our souls'.

We don't have to stretch our minds too far to see how things could be different. There's plenty of research on what happens when the government gives money with no strings attached. Spoiler alert: the 'idle poor' don't hit the Captain Morgan bottle or the casino harder. Indeed, this is an antiquated worldview.

In 1974 'Mincome,' the largest ever basic income experiment, kicked off in a dinky Canadian town 300 kilometres northwest of Winnipeg. A thousand families received monthly checks from the provincial and federal governments to help supplement their earnings. Each family of four, all considered poor, got what today would be equivalent to $19,000 a year. Here's what happened:

> *Hospitalisations decreased*

> *Birth rates dropped*

> *Future generations were positively impacted*

> *Domestic violence declined*

> *Mothers took maternity leave*

> *Young adults postponed getting married*

> *School performance spiked*

> *Mental health improved*

The concern was that free money would disincentivise work. Yet during the four years Mincome was in effect, folks worked about as much as they had before. Other trials in America, England, Kenya, Uganda, Brazil, Namibia, India, Finland, Italy, and the Netherlands show promising results. Yes, there will always be some who play into critics' worst fears, but the vast majority seize the opportunity to create new possibilities. While government services intend to help, they can miss the mark of what a particular person or family requires. People know best what they need, and by taking advantage of the leverage basic income provides, they elevate themselves, their families, and communities.

In one Kenyan trial, an enterprising participant invested his stipend in a motorbike to provide taxi rides, commonly known as a *boda boda*. He then used the profits to set up a small soap business, and then he bought two cows, then opened a barbershop (you get the picture). The potential for creating a vibrant ecosystem of micro-entrepreneurs in developing nations is real. It's in struggling economies where the most valuable applications of basic income may take place. These innovative schemes can improve health and school attendance, reduce crime, and enable countries to become increasingly self-sustaining.

In the Western world, we only have to look at prisons, mental institutes, retraining schools, indigenous reservations, senior homes, ghettos, and halfway houses to see how many are stigmatised and remain permanently out of the job market.

And the American poultry industry is proof that dehumanising jobs are still widespread. The industry sees more finger amputations than any other in the nation. And bathroom breaks are often forbidden, forcing many workers to resort to diapers instead. Meanwhile, we fly 1500 private jets to a Davos Conference to talk about the future of work. Something is fundamentally askew.

The mechanism for rolling out UBI is a complicated one. But when innovative schemes are intrinsically tied to work, they appear to have much better success. Fruitful trials depend on how much money gets doled out, under what conditions, in what frequency, and how it connects to the entire welfare system. Income support, whether embedded within UBI schemes or not, works best when framed in such a way so as to reduce stigma.

It's also concerning that some schemes might be abused. Companies such as McDonald's have aggressively fought minimum wage hikes, expecting their full-time workers to seek social services and food stamps, heating assistance, and other help just to get by. UBI could help justify maintaining a measly McPay. Other corporations could follow suit and weaponise UBI. Anticipating this likelihood with a social safety net could help people retrain and stay in gainful work.

Even deliberating UBI stems from a position of privilege. To entertain a post-work society (a world without jobs) implies that you're doing A-okay. So UBI is first and foremost a proxy to stir debate on a new meaning of work, value, and identity. It's not the solution to the crisis of work. Current welfare systems are riddled with bureaucracy and see people in situations, like in the UK, where you may be better off if you don't work.

Nor is UBI the answer to structural inequality. But at a national level, where basic is relative, schemes show great promise to promote fairness, fuel creativity, and foster entrepreneurship. The social bonds developed between community members leans towards behaviour that elevates the human spirit. And it's the communities that are more resilient that can better identify, support and advance the public good.

Our society must decide if we should all have the opportunity to enjoy the pleasures of a good living. Everybody deserves a basic chance. Whether through UBI or some other means, how we best achieve this is to be determined. A new and better system, imperfect as it will be, is necessary. We must keep searching for ways to repair the world and empower those who will become most vulnerable. It's the only decent thing to do.

BUSINESS AS UNUSUAL

Patagonia founder and shaper extraordinaire Yvon Chouinard lives and breathes better ways of working. His pioneering company is the blueprint for business as unusual. For nearly half a century, the organisation has been in the 'Business of Saving Our Home Planet.'

The business is unusual because it sees value creation and company growth miles apart from the typical shareholder. At a glance, their seemingly counterintuitive policies, like the one that encourages their customers to repair their items instead of buying new ones, creates devout loyalty. In 2018 alone, Patagonia fixed over 100,000 garments. Their 1% for the Planet initiative has raised over 200 million dollars for nonprofit environmental groups, and the company has doubled down on regenerative farming, perhaps the most effective way to store more water and draw more carbon out of the atmosphere. Most extraordinary is the company's paid leave and on-site family care, which has been in place since 1983. Chouinard balances freedom and responsibility so that the company can grow better, not bigger.

Other companies make it a priority to dispense work in a more equitable way, choosing to return more of the means of production (or capital) to workers. Hamdi Ulukaya, the CEO of Chobani Yoghurt, achieved that by making all employees shareholders in the company. This wasn't a public relations stunt or a greedy CEO trying to give back—it was a smart strategy to let people stand on their own two feet. It's why Chobani operates the largest yoghurt facility in the world and has become the sweetheart yoghurt brand of America.

For over a decade the Enspiral Network, a group of social enterprises, businesses, and individuals have taken a radically different approach to work. The collective is living proof that ownership, governance, decisions, and resources can all be more widely and effectively distributed. And as we've seen, when everyone is a leader in a learning organisation like this, it becomes infinitely more resilient.

If more companies operated like Patagonia, Chobani, or Enspiral, we wouldn't be so far up shit creek. 'We are witnessing an erosion of values,' declares shaper Simon Mhanna, 'led by a hunger for power and defiance of our limits as humans. Our response has been mediocre at best.'

Along with several positive deviants companies around the world, new models of innovation and production are taking hold. It forces us to question the continued centrality of firms to the innovation process, advocates Harvard Entrepreneurial and Legal Studies professor Yochai Benkler.

Here's what we could do: instead of platform corporations extracting value to no end, we support platform cooperatives that don't alienate workers or consumers (who really are one and the same). We harness technology and innovation to empower people. Underdogs, whether in food or finance, become top dogs because we become more conscious consumers. We appreciate that growth for its own sake is a disease and that small, indeed, can be beautiful.

While preserving our economy we judicially curb the tax cuts, deregulation, lower tariffs, and financialisation that have facilitated the unbounded growth of the technology titans we see today. Clever company restructuring, 'creative' tax strategies, phony head offices, accelerated depreciation abuse, strategic executive stock buybacks, and offshore tax havens are exposed (or deemed illegal) for the morally fuzzy practices they are. Firms then choose to behave responsibly for both the sake of their reputation and because it's good business.

Indeed, market mechanisms are largely indispensable in our industrial society. But if we don't keep matters in check–whether that be companies scaling too fast for their own good, continued credit default swaps, or big tech takeovers–both the efficiency of the market and our freedom will continue to be under siege.

And it's not just businesses that bear the responsibility. The sea of challenges we face rests on the shoulders of global polity–the private sector and government have a role, as do each of us. Should we get it together, our cultures and social systems will become more resilient. More people will have greater social mobility and be afforded the opportunities to make progress.

Do we need even more evidence to see that changing our course is urgent? Maybe so. The hills in Japan are littered with tsunami stones that warn people not to 'build any homes below this point.' Sometimes builders listen and villages survive a disaster. Other times, signs are ignored and people perish.

We have all the signals we need in front of us right now.

* * *

While our social inequality, economic stagnation, and financial instability might not be enough discomfort to spur a revolution, it has ignited a renaissance. With the vantage of the internet and negligible costs of requisite tools, the means of creative production have been democratised. We now express ourselves on a globally connected stage. We search for alternative forms of meaning, new tools to become enlightened, and novel ways to feel a sense of belonging. It's reflected in our cultural melting pot, art that pushes the envelope, and efforts to solve our most pressing human problems.

This seismic change we're undergoing may seem to be moving like molasses, but with refined time-binding spectacles, we could discern the sweeping shifts happening all around us in this moment. While plants bind light to stay alive and thrive–we bind time to help our descendants flourish. At least that's the idea.

A NEW HORIZON

During the Reagan–Thatcher revolution of the 1980s, the horizon of our shared future began to fade. We entered the age of individualism, and our perceived needs and ego-driven wants reigned supreme. But Gordon Gekko was wrong: greed is not good. Being decent is.

We're still spinning in the aftermath of this special blend of laissez-faire capitalism that jacked up the economy. The 2008 financial crisis presented an opportunity to course-correct that we squandered. In the same vein, this era also perpetuated the falsehood that self-actualisation is an independent affair. But we know that work, as life, is a team sport.

With an infinite number of futures ahead, we could lump them into the plausible, probable, and preferable. Without agreement on the destination to which we should set sail, at the very least we can begin to suss out who's willing to come aboard. Lisa Gill, organisational self-management coach, cautions, 'If we don't have a shared understanding of language then we are trapped in a default future.' And if words can alter how people see things, then things can change.

There will always be unemployment, underemployment, disengagement, and discrimination–but we can still work to make work better. This will require shaping our working lives in unison with each other and continually renewing ourselves in what we do. It means seeking to provide every human with basic needs along with healthcare and education. It's doing our best to ensure that the dignity and opportunities that come with having a livelihood spread to as many people as possible. We can set our sights towards a horizon that advances a system of work that respects all humans, and abides by the golden rule.

The crisis of work is not a problem to be solved. 'We might ease human misery but the battle can't be won—even as real progress is being made, the goal continues to recede,' wrote former U.S. secretary of health, education, and welfare John W. Gardner. What we can do is rewrite our story from this point on—taking a different approach to value creation.

We can measure the wealth of a country by how it performs socially, culturally, and environmentally in addition to how it performs economically. We can acknowledge that it's our intrinsic and social motivations that spark innovation just as much as it is our monetary ones. We can benchmark against how a nation responds to a crisis and looks beyond borders. It's in these times of dissonance that mark the turning points of our collective future.

In the new vista, work is meted out based on both fitness (current skills and capabilities) and needs (future capacities and proper value creation). Caring for family, volunteerism, and community service are valued equally to that of waged work. Courageous leaders step up to guide their organisations and communities down new paths that lift, instead of rob the soul.

We need to concern ourselves not with what could be, but what *should* be.

We can fulfil our purpose and serve the greater good. The preferred future rests on our joint effort to distribute quality work. You can help pave the way.

Choose to open your heart. Engage with the unknown. Resolve to participate.

As shapers, we present our best selves in everyday life. We foster soulful connections with others so we can challenge our assumptions and stretch our thinking. In doing so we remain inspired, express ourselves, develop more compassion, discover more creative solutions, and increase our commitment to take action. We go deep with one another to live, and lead, meaningful lives.

And our time is now.

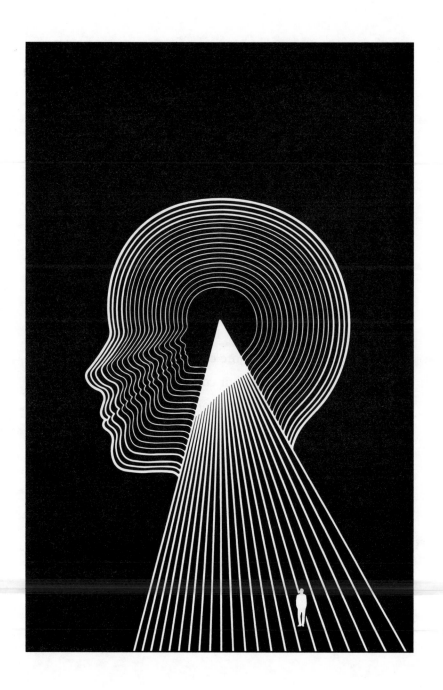

There are no shortcuts to any place worth going

—Beverly Sills

CONCLUSION:
THE SHAPERS LEGACY

Ever so surely work is transforming. It's moving from alienating to fulfilling us. It's shifting from a mode of compliance to one of autonomy. We must be discerning with our energy, manage it like ninjas and at the drop of a hat be ready to change where, when and how we work. The better we know ourselves, the easier it will be to navigate these sea changes with both grace and grit. As shapers, I believe we're in an advantageous position to do just that.

A wave after another will come. And here is how we can sail our ship:

We set ambitious yet realistic priorities and monitor them with regular and balanced input and reflection.

We draw hard-nosed boundaries to remain focused during our most creative hours.

We let go of silly stories and create new and better practices and continually evolve ourselves.

We fine-tune our attention, stay conscious of our moods, stay present and sense what is needed in the moment.

We remain steadfastly accountable to ourselves and to others.

We gain, not lose perspective.

We show up in the world like the people we know we were meant to be.

Working in this fashion–smarter not harder, that is–ain't easy. It forces us to confront our shadow selves, bringing those subconscious parts of us to the surface. We are brave to stretch ourselves well beyond our perceived limits and dare to get uncomfortable. And so, we seek to make our mark on the world.

* * *

The earth is not the centre of the universe, yet until 1543 we functioned as if it were. Likewise, when we ditch the idea that the self is the thing around which everything else rotates, we shift into a new paradigm. Shapers experiment, learn and grow to bring more meaning into their field of view. We renew ourselves by making progress in doing the work that matters most.

We can model our workplaces on classrooms and make them spaces where we're always growing to be better. We can further align our intention with action. With acute self-awareness, sharp intuition and a little heart and soul, we can do the best work of our lives. And once in a while we can just be and not do.

We can see the practice of management as more art than science. We can shape more colourful working lives for ourselves and thereby make the work and the world, more humane. We can share a story of work that addresses the crisis we face and acknowledges the intricate dance between humans, technology and our planet. The question is whether we're willing to paddle out and face the incoming waves.

When we do so, we can live these principles: learning, feeling, leading, becoming and futuring. We can feed our own interests and that of the collective. We transcend by making conscious choices in how we trust, connect and share. It's this partnership that adds flavour to the skyline of our lives.

We act upon our free will not from a place of fear and anxiety but from strength and fullness. We live in cultures of authenticity, propelled forward by our capacity for awe.

Nearly all the world's population growth is taking place in less developed countries, and it's there where the possibilities for work must be created. Through technology, progressive education, career support, skills development and the collective human spirit, our challenge and our duty is to create a new system of work that functions better. For the hundreds of millions of unemployed people on the globe, we need more than 'more jobs.'

The time to make our best contribution is now. Because the future of work is about the meaning we find within it.

Manny wasn't going to turn into a person he didn't want to be. By his own design he's shaped who he has become. Every day he feeds his soul through creative expression. Sure he makes loads of mistakes along the way, but his audacity keeps him moving. He's not worried about failure, only about not trying and regretting it. When we see ourselves like this, as self-renewing individuals—we continue to come alive.

The shaping life works. I really can't imagine doing it any other way. And I'm always in awe of what comes when people I work with transition to become shapers. In discovering meaning and finding flow, they're leaving their stamp on the world.

I'd love to hear from you on how you're shaping things up and the horizon that awaits you.

Visit *www.shapers.life* and share your story.

NOTES

Introduction: A Watershed Moment

Manny is a Shaper, *literally*—**this is what people who make surfboards by hand are called:** An apology in advance to all surfboard shapers. I acknowledge the blood, sweat, and tears that you endure to hone your craft and make a living. Now here I go democratising the title you so rightfully earned. I may burn in hell, but it's a chance I'm willing to take.

PART I: MEANING AND THE NATURE OF WORK

1. The Magic of Meaning

The largest religious group in the USA is 'non-believers.': Cox, D. and Jones, R. P. (2017) 'America's changing religious identity: findings from the 2016 American Values Atlas', *PRRI*, 6 September. Available at: https://www.prri.org/research/american-religious-landscape-christian-religiously-unaffiliated/ (accessed: 16 January 2020).

If happiness is about getting what you want, it appears that meaningfulness is about doing things that express yourself: Baumeister, R. F. (2013) 'The meaning of life', *Aeon*, 16 September. Available at: https://aeon.co/essays/what-is-better-a-happy-life-or-a-meaningful-one (accessed: 10 January 2020).

In a large international study of the most meaningful things in life, work was mentioned 44% of the time, ranking second only to that of family: Fullagar, C. and Fave, A. D. (eds) (2017) *Flow at Work: Measurement and Implications.* Routledge.

'This obligation is both spiritual and material, in that no matter what it is, the shokunin's responsibility is to fulfil the requirement': Juma, A. (2017) 'Shokunin and sushi: what jiro can teach us about mastery', *Medium*, 6 October. Available at: https://medium.com/@alyjuma/shokunin-and-sushi-what-jiro-can-teach-us-about-mastery-1a886f129df4 (accessed: 10 January 2020).

Japanese workers have pep in their step: A generalisation to be sure. And this also sets aside many ailments like job shortages, lack of feedback in the workplace, not firing unfit employees, the threat of advanced artificial intelligence, and the unchecked power of bosses to name a few. Still, with my foreign eyes, these are all overshadowed by the spirited Japanese work ethic and *can-do attitude.*

In Japan, there is the cultural conformity to give everything you got to whatever it is you do: Indeed, this also why upwards of a million individuals have completely withdrawn from society. *Hikikomori,* as they are known, have turned inwards and become 'post-modern hermits' amid the pressures of life.

It's precisely why of all the businesses worldwide that have been around for over 100 years, 90% are Japanese: Matsuyama, T. (2019) 'I stopped setting a financial goal for my SaaS', *Medium*, 16 October. Available at: https://blog.inkdrop.info/i-stopped-setting-a-financial-goal-for-my-saas-a92c3db65506 (accessed: 10 January 2020).

More folks could take a cue from the Japanese where good work, good business, and good citizenry for that matter, envelop a deep personal commitment to making your best contribution: Of course there are some perils of this which we will encounter later on; *karoshi* (death by overworking), workaholism, and often a terrible work–life balance to name some.

They are also locked in mortal combat: de Botton, A. (2018) *The Sorrows of Work*. The School of Life.

Never before has the burden on the self been so damn heavy: Perel, E. (2019) *Famed Relationship Therapist Esther Perel Gives Advice on Intimacy, Careers, and Self-Improvement*. Available at: https://www.youtube.com/watch?v=QFwWvr1YUjA (accessed: 10 January 2020).

That we feel disillusioned when the career ladder has collapsed and our attempts to impact our communities and leave a mark on the world has become more challenging?: Claman, P. (2012) 'There is no career ladder', *Harvard Business Review*, 14 February. Available at: https://hbr.org/2012/02/there-is-no-career-ladder (accessed: 10 January 2020).

2. A Short History of Work

We've even come up with a snazzy name for this era: the Fourth Industrial Revolution: Schwab, K. (2016) *The Fourth Industrial Revolution: what it means and how to respond*, World Economic Forum. Available at: https://www.weforum.org/agenda/2016/01/the-fourth-industrial-revolution-what-it-means-and-how-to-respond/ (accessed: 1 October 2019).

Features a psychological contract and a veil of security: MacKenzie2006, Bob. "What Is a Psychological Contract?" *What Is a Psychological Contract?*, 2020. Available at: www.alchemyformanagers.co.uk/topics/6ixdhhPwDvZFjsZc.html.

Similarly, today, in the spirit of capitalism and economic self-interest, we seek salvation through an 'orgy of materialism': 'In an orgy of materialism,' see Weber, M. (2013) *The Protestant Ethic and the Spirit of Capitalism*. Abridged edition. United States: Merchant Books.

Individual control over the techniques and quantity of personal production began to fade with the rise of automation: Gilbert, J. B. (1977) *Work without Salvation*. Baltimore: The Johns Hopkins University Press.

It lent well into a straight shot of overtime, wage increases, and benefits still keenly protected: Frase, P. (2016) *Four Futures: Life After Capitalism*. London: Verso, p. 15; Rifkin, J. (2018) *The Third Industrial Revolution: Can we prevent the next mass extinction of life on Earth?* Available at: https://www.youtube .com/watch?v=BwrkajhEvxw (accessed: 1 October 2019).

Because, for the first time ever, we would own the 'technology of consciousness': Toffler, A. (1984) *Future Shock*. Reissue edition. New York: Bantam.

Organisational theorist Ikujiro Nonaka, another pioneer shaper, wanted to help managers appreciate how knowledge—the fuel for innovation—could be leveraged: 'Knowledge worker' (2019) *Wikipedia*. Available at: https:// en.wikipedia.org/w/index.php?title=Knowledge_worker™oldid=915770921 (accessed: 2 October 2019).

Indeed, the information economy is growing and the wave of knowledge workers continues to swell higher: Zumbrun, J. (2016) 'The rise of knowledge workers is accelerating despite the threat of automation', *The Wall Street Journal*, 4 May. Available at: https://blogs.wsj.com/economics/2016/05/ 04/the-rise-of-knowledge-workers-is-accelerating-despite-the-threat-of-automation/ (accessed: 2 October 2019).

The most important weapon for businesses today is the ability to empower their workers: Bradley, A. J. and McDonald, M. P. (2011) 'People are not your greatest asset', *Harvard Business Review*, 6 December. Available at: https:// hbr.org/2011/12/people-are-not-your-greatest-a (accessed: 2 October 2019).

A whopping 40% of Americans are 'liquid asset poor', or—in plain English—just one paycheck away from poverty: Bach, N. (2019) 'Millions of Americans are one missed paycheck away from poverty, report says', *Fortune*, 29 January. Available at: https://fortune.com/2019/01/29/americans-liquid-asset-poor-propserity-now-report/ (accessed: 2 October 2019).

We long to give life to any or all of our multitudinous selves: de Botton, *The Sorrows of Work*.

'New capitalism' becomes a new way for us to think about ourselves, our work and our life: Pranz, S. (2017) 'Economy of self-exploitation',

Anxy, 31 October. Available at: https://sebastianpranz.de/economy-of-self-exploitation/ (accessed: 2 October 2019).

And now, at last, shapers are able to direct their own energies and remove the shackles that restricted the possibility for meaningful work: Bradley, H. (1998) *Gender and Power in the Workplace: Analysing the Impact of Economic Change.* New York: Palgrave.

3. Employee Disengagement Epidemic

But nearly half of Americans now work in non-routine, cognitively demanding jobs: Zumbrun, 'The rise of knowledge workers is accelerating'.

They must face the stark reality that their jobs, as anthropologist David Graeber puts it, could be bullshit: Glaser, E. (2018) 'Bullshit Jobs: A Theory by David Graeber review – the myth of capitalist efficiency', *The Guardian*, 25 May. Available at: https://www.theguardian.com/books/2018/may/25/bullshit-jobs-a-theory-by-david-graeber-review (accessed: 2 October 2019); Heller, N. (2018) 'The bullshit-job boom', *The New Yorker*, 7 June. Available at: https://www.newyorker.com/books/under-review/the-bullshit-job-boom (accessed: 2 October 2019). A simple test to see if you have a meaningful job (and perhaps more importantly if you see it as such) is whether you do work so obviously useful you only need describe it. Graeber cites middle managers, many administrative roles, PR professionals, and corporate lawyers as holding bullshit jobs.

Still others might actually possess meaningful work but be in the odd frame of mind where they just don't feel it: There is a line of thinking that many don't actually want to be useful but merely want to feel useful. Automation then, as it exposes inefficiencies, is a crisis of these feelings that can provide for an existential opening.

At the time of writing, Gallup reports that a whopping 85% of the world's 1 billion full-time employees are not engaged in their work: Gallup, Inc *Engage Your Employees to See High Performance and Innovation, Gallup .com.* Available at: https://www.gallup.com/workplace/229424/employee-engagement.aspx (accessed: 2 October 2019).

Monday through Friday sort of dying: Terkel, S. (1997) *Working: People Talk About What They Do All Day and How They Feel About What They Do*. New York: The New Press, p. xi.

There's nothing distinctively unusual about *not working* at work: This is borrowed from Finnish artist Pilvi Takal and her performance piece *The Trainee*. While at Deloitte she would stare into space doing nothing or ride the elevators up and down telling her colleagues she was doing thought work. From: Odell, Jenny. *How to do Nothing: Resisting the Attention Economy*. S.l.: Melville House, 2020.

In one French study, a CEO said that 19% of his workers were so disengaged that they were planning to sabotage the organisation—they disliked it that much (they didn't act for fear of losing their jobs): Microsoft News Center (2016) *The future of work, Microsoft*. Available at: https://news.microsoft.com/features/futureofwork/ (accessed: 2 October 2019).

Indeed, emotional states play a part in every facet of our working lives—from what we contribute through to how we might feel a sense of belonging: Fosslien, L. and Duffy, M. W. (2019) *No Hard Feelings: The Secret Power of Embracing Emotions at Work*. New York, NY: Portfolio.

Put into a financial context, the estimated savings from firing (or avoiding the hiring of a toxic employee) is $12,489: Housman, M. and Minor, D. (2015) *Toxic Workers*. Harvard Business School Working Paper 16–057. Rochester, NY: HSB. Available at: https://papers.ssrn.com/abstract=2677700 (accessed: 2 October 2019).

And disengaged workers (often found to have traces of toxicity) cost the American economy alone $350 billion per year in lost productivity: Haydon, R. (2013) *Show Me the Money: The Bottom Line Impact of Employee Engagement, TLNT*. Available at: https://www.tlnt.com/show-me-the-money-the-bottom-line-impact-of-employee-engagement/ (accessed: 2 October 2019).

Engaged workers are less likely to have accidents, take sick days, make mistakes, behave badly with co-workers and family, burnout, or suffer from depression than their disengaged counterparts: Nink, M. and Robinson, J.

(2016) *Can Bad Managers Be Saved?*, *Gallup.com*. Available at: https://www
.gallup.com/workplace/236402/bad-managers-saved.aspx (accessed: 2 October 2019).

Take email for starters. On average, 77% of workers surveyed in the UK claim that a productive day is 'clearing their email' and 40% say that four or more hours of 'doing email' is a good day's work: *Ibid.* (Microsoft)

The biggest stoke in work is whether you believe you're making headway in purposeful work: Amabile, T. *Teresa Amabile's Progress Principle, The Progress Principle*. Available at: http://progressprinciple.com/research (accessed: 2 October 2019).

High on the list of making progress in work is gaining a sense of appreciation to keep you motivated: Glei, J. K. (2016) 'A sense of appreciation is the single most sustainable motivator at work', *Jocelyn K. Glei*, 3 August. Available at: https://jkglei.com/appreciation/ (accessed: 2 October 2019).

For many folks, those stories that once conjured up anxiety and dread might soon be seen as existential openings: 'Andrew J. Taggart—Existential Openings & Psychotechnologies of Self-Transformation by Emerge: Making Sense of What's Next • A Podcast on Anchor'. Anchor. Accessed April 4, 2020. https://anchor.fm/emerge/episodes/Andrew-J--Taggart---Existential-Openings--Psychotechnologies-of-Self-Transformation-ebegru.

4. Inhumane Resources

Third-wave workers 'Seek meaning along with financial reward', declared Alvin Toffler over 40 years ago: Case, S. (2017) *The Third Wave: An Entrepreneur's Vision of the Future*. New, Expanded edition. New York: Simon & Schuster.

'Adam Smith's ideas about human nature were much more invention than discovery. His argument for what people were like were false. But they gave rise to a process of industrialisation that made them true': Schwartz, B. (2015b) '"Wealth of Nations" stole happiness from workers – here's how we steal it back.' Available at: https://qz.com/531996/wealth-of-nations-stole-happiness-from-workers-heres-how-we-steal-it-back/ (accessed: 2 October 2019); Schwartz, B. (2015c) *Why We Work*. New York: Simon & Schuster/TED.

In modelling our workplace on the thesis that people are inherently lazy and spurred solely by dangling carrots, we turned a myth into a reality: For more on false theories of work turned true, see Schwartz, *Why We Work*, p. 74.

Purposeful work is a responsibility because it betters yourself and society: Schwartz, B. (2015a) 'Rethinking work', *The New York Times*, 28 August. Available at: https://www.nytimes.com/2015/08/30/opinion/sunday/rethinking-work.html (accessed: 2 October 2019).

A *good jobs strategy* is one that makes a long-term investment in people through better pay, ongoing training, and the intrinsic motivation that comes with autonomy: Ton, Z. (2014) *The Good Jobs Strategy: How the Smartest Companies Invest in Employees to Lower Costs and Boost Profits*. 1st edition. Amazon Publishing.

It's also the main reason why the model of neighbourhood care is going global: Brindle, D. (2017) 'Buurtzorg: the Dutch model of neighbourhood care that is going global', *The Guardian*, 9 May. Available at: https://www.theguardian.com/social-care-network/2017/may/09/buurtzorg-dutch-model-neighbourhood-care (accessed: 1 October 2019).

If a potential candidate is rude to the driver on the way to the interview, you can be sure that Jack or Jill ain't getting that gig: Tatley, K. (2015) 'Zappos – hiring for culture and the bizarre things they do', *The RecruitLoop*, 13 July. Available at: https://recruitloop.com/blog/zappos-hiring-for-culture-and-the-bizarre-things-they-do/ (accessed: 2 October 2019).

In 2014, leading pharmacy, CVS, decided to stop selling cigarettes: 'CVS stops selling tobacco – message from Larry Merlo' (2014) *CVS Health*. Available at: https://cvshealth.com/thought-leadership/message-from-larry-merlo-president-and-ceo (accessed: 2 October 2019).

The airline industry is often criticised for grumpy employees and poor customer service (and, yes, sometimes even dragging uncooperative passengers off the plane): 'United Express Flight 3411 incident' (2019) *Wikipedia*.

Available at: https://en.wikipedia.org/w/index.php?title=United_Express_ Flight_3411_incident&oldid=917763376 (accessed: 2 October 2019).

Regardless of the pressure to expand, the behemoth only grew if it could simultaneously uphold company values: Schlanger, D. (2012) *How Southwest Keeps Making Money In A Brutal Airline Industry, Business Insider.* Available at: https://www.businessinsider.com/case-study-how-southwest-stays-profitable-2012-6 (accessed: 2 October 2019).

At the Ritz Carlton, well known for giving up to $2000 per employee to spend on customer delight, it can get you promoted: Hurn, C. (2012) 'Stuffed giraffe shows what customer service is all about', *HuffPost*, 17 May. Available at: https://www.huffpost.com/entry/stuffed-giraffe-shows-wha_b_ 1524038 (accessed: 25 September 2019).

It's not debatable, but a basic reality of human nature: Schwartz, *Why We Work.*

Nearly half of all US workers are now millennials and by 2025, that percentage will jump to 75%: Deloitte (2014) *Big demands and high expectations: The Deloitte Millennial Survey.* Deloitte. Available at: https:// www2.deloitte.com/mu/en/pages/about-deloitte/articles/2014-millennial-survey-positive-impact.html (accessed: 30 September 2019); 'Millennials dominate the workforce & driving shifts in the workplace' (2018) *Memoori*, 30 August. Available at: https://memoori.com/millennials-now-dominate-workforce-driving-tectonic-shifts-workplace/ (accessed: 30 September 2019); PricewaterhouseCoopers *Workforce of the Future: The Competing Forces Shaping 2030.* PwC, p. 42. Available at: https://www.pwc.com/gx/en/services/ people-organisation/workforce-of-the-future/workforce-of-the-future-the-competing-forces-shaping-2030-pwc.pdf (accessed: 2 October 2019).

5. The Drive to Work

Yet Maslow never intended the path to personal bliss to be so quaintly staged, nor to be represented as a pyramid: Kaufman, S. B. (2019) 'Who created Maslow's iconic pyramid?', *Scientific American Blog Network*, 23

April. Available at: https://blogs.scientificamerican.com/beautiful-minds/who-created-maslows-iconic-pyramid/ (accessed: 2 October 2019).

With their self-determination theory, Edward Deci and Richard Ryan built upon Maslow's work. Here, motivation rests on three innate psychological needs that shape our behaviour: 1) competence, 2) relatedness, and 3) autonomy: David, L. (2014) 'Self-determination theory (Deci and Ryan)', *Learning Theories*, 16 July. Available at: https://www.learning-theories.com/self-determination-theory-deci-and-ryan.html (accessed: 2 October 2019).

More recently, Barry Schwartz and organisational psychologist Amy Wrzesniewski found that work activities can have internal and instrumental *consequences* but this doesn't necessarily mean that those who thrive at work have internal and instrumental *motives*: Wrzesniewski, A. and Schwartz, B. (2014) 'The secret of effective motivation', *The New York Times*, 4 July. Available at: https://www.nytimes.com/2014/07/06/opinion/sunday/the-secret-of-effective-motivation.html (accessed: 2 October 2019).

And although there is no one-size-fits-all solution for a company, we can think in systems with the interconnectedness of control, context, and collaboration: The concepts/principles are gleaned from Steelcase's Engagement and the Global Workplace Report, spanning 17 countries and nearly 13 000 participants. Steelcase Inc. (2016) *Engagement and the Global Workplace: Key findings to amplify the performance of people, teams and organizations*. Available at: http://cdn2.hubspot.net/hubfs/1822507/2016-WPR/Americas/Final_Digital_PDF.pdf?__hssc=130454992.1.1570019037938&__hstc=130454992.0d2f1051f9eb97a06609f88b46657fea.1570019037936.15700 19037936.1570019037936.1&hsCtaTracking=7f761c46-6062-436e-824a-e3a1 a252b89c%7C6ccb9a82-f9ce-4b49-9afb-f030459d27b9.

What's needed in turn way of working that champions cognitive and cultural diversity, multiple opinions, and a knack for adapting to change: Goings, R. (2016) 'Is the meaning of work about to change?', *World Economic Forum*. Available at: https://www.weforum.org/agenda/2016/02/beyond-jobs-beyond-corporations-the-collaboration-economy/ (accessed: 2 October 2019).

When we sync with our motivations, we can discover more meaning, build better organisations, and weave a richer social fabric: Mead, M. (2001) *Sex and Temperament: In Three Primitive Societies*. New York: Harper Perennial.

6. Work-Life Blend

In all of these roles I was a *segmentor*: work was work and I got my kicks in life and satisfaction elsewhere: Fessler, L. (2018) 'Are you an integrator or a segmentor? Knowing the answer helps with work-life balance', *Quartz at Work*, 8 August. Available at: https://qz.com/work/1349189/are-you-an-integrator-or-a-segmentor-knowing-the-answer-can-help-with-work-life-balance/ (accessed: 30 September 2019).

And we're now witnessing passionate job quitters and an entire gamut of flexible working arrangements help shape the *Great Migration*: Gershon, I. (2017) 'How work changed to make us all passionate quitters', *Aeon*, 26 July. Available at: https://aeon.co/essays/how-work-changed-to-make-us-all-passionate-quitters (accessed: 30 September 2019).

An expert on the boundaries between work and life, Rothbard explains that when we find meaning in our work—seeing it as a joyous endeavour—we don't necessarily need to recover like 'unhappy workaholics': Fessler, 'Are you an integrator or a segmentor?'

Japanese authorities declared it death by *karoshi*: McCurry, J. (2017) 'Japanese woman "dies from overwork" after logging 159 hours of overtime in a month', *The Guardian*, 5 October. Available at: https://www.theguardian.com/world/2017/oct/05/japanese-woman-dies-overwork-159-hours-overtime (accessed: 1 October 2019).

This trend epitomises what German philosopher Joseph Pieper called *total work*—when humans become workers and nothing else: Taggart, Andrew. 'If Work Dominated Your Every Moment Would Life Be Worth Living? – Andrew Taggart: Aeon Ideas'. *Aeon*, Aeon, 20 Dec. 2017, aeon.co/ideas/if-work-dominated-your-every-moment-would-life-be-worth-living.

We'll need to slip seamlessly among creative, experimental, risky, emotive, collaborative, analytical, and networked mindsets and functions: Störmer, E. *et al.* (2014) *The Future of Work: Jobs and Skills in 2030.* Evidence Report 84. UK Commission for Employment and Skills, p. 198. Available at: https:// assets.publishing.service.gov.uk/government/uploads/system/uploads/attach ment_data/file/303334/er84-the-future-of-work-evidence-report.pdf; Schwab, *The Fourth Industrial Revolution.*

Instead of focusing on a particular genre of opera, the most successful composers cross-train, pulling from a rich mix of genres: Kaufman, S. B. (2016) 'Creativity is much more than 10,000 hours of deliberate practice', *Scientific American,* 17 April. Available at: https://blogs.scientificamerican .com/beautiful-minds/creativity-is-much-more-than-10-000-hours-of- deliberate-practice/ (accessed: 1 October 2019).

In another instance, excessive schooling impaired creativity in writers who received a lot of formal education: Frensch, P. A. and Sternberg, R. J. (1989) 'Expertise and intelligent thinking: When is it worse to know better?', in Sternberg, R. J. (ed.) *Advances in the Psychology of Human Intelligence.* Hillsdale, NJ, US: Lawrence Erlbaum Associates, Inc, pp. 157–188.

It's in the *antidisciplinary* space, where a certain field is yet to exist, that the magic happens: Ito, J. (2014) 'Antidisciplinary', *MIT Media Lab Blog,* 2. Available at: https://joi.ito.com/weblog/2014/10/02/antidisciplinar.html (accessed: 10 January 2020).

Too much expertise can actually be detrimental to creative greatness: Kaufman, 'Creativity is much more than 10,000 hours of deliberate practice'.

PART II: BETTER WAYS OF WORKING

7. Bad Bosses

Research from MIT demonstrates that, while the quality of leadership is rarely mentioned when people talk about meaningful moments at work, bad management is the 'top destroyer of meaningfulness': Bailey, C. and

Madden, A. (2016) 'What makes work meaningful—or meaningless', *MIT Sloan Management Review*, 1 June. Available at: https://sloanreview.mit.edu/article/what-makes-work-meaningful-or-meaningless/ (accessed: 2 October 2019).

It contributes to serious physical issues including depression, high blood pressure, weight gain, substance abuse, and even premature death: DeCaro, M. S. *et al.* (2011) 'Choking under pressure: Multiple routes to skill failure', *Journal of Experimental Psychology: General*, 140(3), pp. 390–406. doi: 10.1037/a0023466; Gonzalez-Mule, E. (2016) 'Worked to death? IU study says little control over high-stress jobs can lead to early grave', *IU Bloomington Newsroom*. Available at: http://news.indiana.edu/releases/iu/2016/10/worked-to-death-job-control-mortality.shtml (accessed: 2 October 2019); Beall, A. (2017) 'How a toxic boss could ruin your career', *Daily Mail Online*, 6 January. Available at: http://www.dailymail.co.uk/~/article-4092054/index.html (accessed: 2 October 2019).

The real shocker is that most of those captains at the helm of the company ship don't have what it takes to be a 21st century leader: Adkins, A. (2015) 'Only One in 10 People Possess the Talent to Manage', *Gallup.com*. Available at: https://www.gallup.com/workplace/236579/one-people-possess-talent-manage.aspx (accessed: 1 October 2019); Ungerboeck, K. (2017) 'Silicon Valley has idolized Steve Jobs for decades—and it's finally paying the price,' *Quartz*. Available at: https://qz.com/984174/silicon-valley-has-idolized-steve-jobs-for-decades-and-its-finally-paying-the-price/ (accessed: 2 October 2019).

Once thought to be a light-hearted theory at best, new evidence proves this principle to be very real: Wagner, R. (2018) 'New evidence the Peter Principle is real—and what to do about it', *Forbes*, 10 April. Available at: https://www.forbes.com/sites/roddwagner/2018/04/10/new-evidence-the-peter-principle-is-real-and-what-to-do-about-it/ (accessed: 2 October 2019).

This breed of leader, as we'll see in Chapter 16, seeks to enrich the working spirit rather than quash it: Altman, J. (2018a) 'Four models for a modern leader', *Quartz at Work*, 4 May. Available at: https://qz.com/work/1270483/

management-today-requires-these-four-types-of-leadership/ (accessed: 25 September 2019).

'Having the freedom to work where you want, in your own time, rather than among people and in a place not of your choosing, are things that people increasingly value, and not only those at the top end of the pay-scale': Skidelsky, W. (2017) 'A job for life: the "new economy" and the rise of the artisan career', *Financial Times*, 21 April. Available at: https://www.ft.com/content/c2d971bc-24f5-11e7-a34a-538b4cb30025 (accessed: 2 October 2019).

Social psychologist Douglas McGregor categorises leaders into two distinct types: Mind Tools Content Team *Theory X and Theory Y: Understanding People's Motivations*. Available at: http://www.mindtools.com/pages/article/newLDR_74.htm (accessed: 2 October 2019).

More and more we are seeing how workers are motivated by the results they might achieve as well as intrinsic benefits: Ariely, D. (2012) *What makes us feel good about our work?* (TEDxRiodelaPlata). Available at: https://www.ted.com/talks/dan_ariely_what_makes_us_feel_good_about_our_work (accessed: 2 October 2019).

8. The Pursuit of Dopeness

Likewise, dopeness can be realised through small gains and the commitment to continuously learn, practise, and improve: Or as Alvin Toffler put it much more eloquently: 'The illiterate of the 21st century will not be those who cannot read and write, but those who cannot learn, unlearn, and relearn.' Toffler, A. (1984) *The Third Wave*. New York, NY: Bantam.

We need to put an end to the God-awful habit of multitasking. It's proven to make us less efficient: Levitin, D. J. (2015) 'Why the modern world is bad for your brain', *The Observer*, 18 January. Available at: https://www.theguardian.com/science/2015/jan/18/modern-world-bad-for-brain-daniel-j-levitin-organized-mind-information-overload (accessed: 2 October 2019).

We're fracturing our attention because we're still thinking of the previous task when we embark on the new one: Basu, T. (2016) 'Something called "attention residue" is ruining your concentration', *The Cut*, 21 January. Available at: https://www.thecut.com/2016/01/attention-residue-is-ruining-your-concentration.html (accessed: 2 October 2019).

'Either way, your output level suffers, as does the quality of your work': Telis, G. (2010) 'Multitasking splits the brain', *Science | AAAS*, 15 April. Available at: https://www.sciencemag.org/news/2010/04/multitasking-splits-brain (accessed: 2 October 2019); Stulberg, B. (2017) 'to get better at time management, borrow a training strategy from elite athletes', *The Cut*, 25 May. Available at: https://www.thecut.com/article/high-intensity-interval-training-work-productivity-breaks.html (accessed: 1 October 2019).

With over 175 cognitive biases at play, your own story of your place in the world is inherently skewed by how you choose to see things: Benson, B. (2019) 'Cognitive bias cheat sheet,' *Medium*. Available at: https://medium.com/better-humans/cognitive-bias-cheat-sheet-55a472476b18 (accessed: 2 October 2019).

When it comes down to motivation the trick is to find ways to continually inspire yourself: Fosslien and Duffy, *No Hard Feelings*, p. 50.

It'll likely happen only for some, over time, and probably through small wins: Amabile, T. and Kramer, S. J. (2011) 'The power of small wins', *Harvard Business Review*, 1 May. Available at: https://hbr.org/2011/05/the-power-of-small-wins (accessed: 2 October 2019).

While we've seen that why we work is for both intrinsic and instrumental rewards, it's internal motivations that can have the greatest impact on performance: Wrzesniewski and Schwartz, 'The secret of effective motivation.'

The concept, developed by psychologists Amy Wrzesniewski and Jane E. Dutton, involves taking the components of your job and redesigning them to better align with your talent and interests through a three-tiered framework: Wrzesniewski, A. and Dutton, J. (2001) 'Crafting a job: revisioning employees as active crafters of their work', *Academy of Management Review*, 26(2), pp. 179–201. doi: 10.2307/259118.

When the values of the individual align with their work, meaning can ensue, providing variety, autonomy, challenge, feedback on performance, and the opportunity to see progress: Grant, A. (2014) 'The no. 1 feature of a meaningless job', Available at: http://www.psychologytoday.com/blog/give-and-take/201401/the-no-1-feature-meaningless-job (accessed: 2 October 2019).

When having five different careers in a lifetime is now standard, and even advised by the *Financial Times,* the road once less travelled is now bumper to bumper: Barrett, H. (2017) 'Plan for five careers in a lifetime', *Financial Times,* 5 September. Available at: https://www.ft.com/content/0151d2fe-868a-11e7-8bb1-5ba57d47eff7 (accessed: 2 October 2019).

9.   Vital Ingredients

And his toolbox is mighty big: Kamp, D. (2013) 'The cat's meow', *Vanity Fair,* 13 December. Available at: https://www.vanityfair.com/hollywood/2013/01/martin-short-hollywoods-most-beloved (accessed: 1 October 2019).

Cultivating fluidity means seeking change, continuously improving, all the while expertly navigating towards a future that's only coming at us faster: Ito, J. and Howe, J. (2016) *Whiplash: How to Survive Our Faster Future.* New York, NY: Grand Central Publishing.

Google boasts more contractors than full-timers, with an average employee tenure of just 1.1 years: Woods, N. and Rafaeli, J. S. (2016) *Good Cop, Bad War.* Ebury Press.

10.   Fluid Teams Work

Effective teams need clear goals, well-defined tasks, the right skills and experience at hand, sufficient resources, and access to support: Hackman, J. R. (2002) *Leading Teams: Setting the Stage for Great Performances.* 1st edition. Boston, MA: Harvard Business Review Press.

'They have been able to combine a realistic view of the often-temporary nature of the employment relationship with a focus on shared goals and long-term personal relationships ... teams win when their individual members trust each other enough to prioritize team success over individual glory': Hoffman, R., Casnocha, B., and Yeh, C. (2014) 'Your company is not a family', *Harvard Business Review*, 17 June. Available at: https://hbr.org/2014/06/your-company-is-not-a-family (accessed: 1 October 2019).

Effective *teaming*, then, is really the knack for collaborating in fluid groupings: Edmondson, A. C. (2012) 'Teamwork on the fly', *Harvard Business Review*, 1 April. Available at: https://hbr.org/2012/04/teamwork-on-the-fly-2 (accessed: 1 October 2019).

Since 2001, they have been innovating with people and teams outside of their company: P&G 'Do you have the next game changing innovation?', *P&G*. Available at: https://www.pgconnectdevelop.com/ (accessed: 1 October 2019).

Started in 2006, the goal was to find a better algorithm to help predict which movie you might enjoy (in case you're curious, the first winner was a team led by AT&T engineers called 'Belkor's Pragmatic Chaos'): Prizemaster (2009) *Netflix Prize: Forum*. Available at: https://www.netflixprize.com/community/topic_1537.html (accessed: 1 October 2019).

From something as trivial as Walker's Snack Food company crowdsourcing new chip flavours (Crispy Duck and Hoisin flavour anyone?) through to something as serious as Bill and Melinda Gates Foundation's Global Grand Challenge to create a toilet of the future, great ideas can come from anywhere: *Mirror* (2018) 'Futuristic toilet that transforms human poo into fertiliser', 6 November. Available at: https://www.mirror.co.uk/science/bill-gates-reveals-futuristic-toilet-13541719 (accessed: 1 October 2019).

'More and more people in nearly every industry are now working on multiple teams that vary in duration, have a constantly shifting membership, and pursue moving targets': Edmondson, 'Teamwork on the fly.'

Buurtzorg uses under 40% of the hours that Dutch doctors have stipulated for patient care, reduces all emergency hospital visits by 30%, and saves the Dutch healthcare system hundreds of millions of euros every year:

'About Buurtzorg International' *Buurtzorg International.* Available at: https://www.buurtzorg.com/about-us/ (accessed: 1 October 2019).

In the business world, effective *teaming* helped Airbnb enter the Cuban market in just 10 weeks: Golden, J. (2016) 'The power of the elastic product team—airbnb's first pm on how to build your own', *Firstround.com.* Available at: /review/the-power-of-the-elastic-product-team-airbnbs-first-pm-on-how-to-build-your-own/ (accessed: 1 October 2019).

Over time, and with the advantage of thousands of stores, notable trends emerge: Grupo Inditex the umbrella of brands like ZARA, Massimo Dutti, Pull & Bear, Bershka and more boasts, 420 stores in 202 markets. Inditex 'Who we are,' *inditex.com.* Available at: https://www.inditex.com/about-us/who-we-are (accessed: 1 October 2019).

The shop employees dub their customers 'bosses': In one case, an employee recommended that it would be wise to place all the stew vegetables near the meat sections. In this way bosses could get all the ingredients they needed a stew much faster. This is the type of initiative to be expected when workers are empowered and able to manage themselves. See Ton, *The Good Jobs Strategy.*

'Beautiful organisations keep asking questions, they remain incomplete': Leberecht, T. (2016) '4 ways to build a human company in the age of machines' (*TEDSummit*). Available at: https://www.ted.com/talks/tim_leberecht_4_ways_to_build_a_human_company_in_the_age_of_machines (accessed: 1 October 2019).

11.   Managing Self-Management

'In the past, you had control through compliance. In the future, you're going to have control through transparency, social pressure, and responsibility': Ludolph, E. (2019) 'Aaron Dignan: being a leader means giving up control', *Adobe 99U*, 19 March. Available at: https://99u.adobe.com/articles/62745/aaron-dignan-being-a-leader-means-giving-up-control (accessed: 1 October 2019).

And while it may not suit everyone, the benefits of self-management are hard to argue against: more engaged, happy, creative, and collaborative: Gill, L. (2018) '10 components that successfully abolished hierarchy (in 70+ Companies)', *Corporate Rebels*, 22 March. Available at: https://corporate-rebels.com/10-components-k2k/ (accessed: 1 October 2019).

Oh yes, let's not forget that self-managed organisations are way more efficient with at least a 35 percent boost to productivity: 'Ep. 33 Margaret Wheatley on Leadership and Warriors for the Human Spirit'. *Leadermorphosis.* (accessed April 4, 2020). http://leadermorphosis.co/ep-33-margaret-wheatley-on-leadership-and-warriors-for-the-human-spirit; Weisbord, Marvin. 'Productive workplaces: Dignity, meaning, and community in the 21st century'. *Amazon.* Jossey-Bass, 2012. https://www.amazon.com/Productive-Workpla ces-Dignity-Meaning-Community/dp/0470900172.

Self-management cultures treat employees like adults so they can shape their own work. They freely collaborate with colleagues, manage their own time, and make conscious decisions on how to best contribute: McCord, P. (2014) 'How Netflix reinvented HR', *Harvard Business Review*, 1 January. Available at: https://hbr.org/2014/01/how-netflix-reinvented-hr (accessed: 25 September 2019).

The best way to manage yourself is to know yourself: Drucker, P. F. (2005) 'Managing oneself', *Harvard Business Review*, 1 January. Available at: https://hbr.org/2005/01/managing-oneself (accessed: 1 October 2019).

More importantly, it sent a message: 'We trust you': Semler, R. (2014) 'How to run a company with (almost) no rules' (*TEDGlobal 2014*). Available at: https://www.ted.com/talks/ricardo_semler_how_to_run_a_company_with_almost_no_rules (accessed: 1 October 2019).

Under his leadership Semco grew from $4million in revenue in 1982 to over $212 million in 2003: 'Ricardo Semler'. *Wikipedia.* Wikimedia Foundation, January 7, 2019. https://en.wikipedia.org/wiki/Ricardo_Semler.

More impressively perhaps, is their employee turnover rates that have been less than one percent: Cooper, Cary L., and Ronald J. Burke. *Reinventing HRM: Challenges and New Directions.* London: Routledge, 2005.

Today effective managers are a rare breed—only 1 out of every 10 have what it takes to be a courageous leader: Adkins, *Only One in 10 People Possess the Talent to Manage.*

Through the advice process, workers use their creativity and problem-solving abilities to do what they deem best: *Decision Making Reinventing Organizations Wiki.* Available at: http://www.reinventingorganizationswiki.com/ Decision_Making (accessed: 4 March 2020).

A lot like Chinese consumer electronics company Haier: Minnaar, J. and de Morree, P. (2018) 'The world's most pioneering company of our times', *Corporate Rebels,* 31 January. Available at: https://corporate-rebels.com/ haier/ (accessed: 1 October 2019).

They've banished nearly 10 000 middle managers and reorganised into an ecosystem of startups where employees function as entrepreneurs: *Ibid.*

Spotify has its unique brew of self-management and so does tomato processor Morning Start and blogging platform Medium: Brindle, 'Buurtzorg: the Dutch model of neighbourhood care that is going global'.

It's a recipe that should be modelled by others but made wholly their own: Cabraal, A. and Basterfield, S. (2019) *Better Work Together: How the Power of Community Can Transform Your Business.* Auckland, New Zealand: Enspiral Foundation Limited.

In 2013, when Zappos made the move to Holocracy (the former flag bearer of the self-management movement), 29% of the company's staff abandoned ship: Reingold, J. (2016) 'How a radical shift left Zappos reeling', *Fortune,* 4 March. Available at: https://fortune.com/longform/zappos-tony-hsieh-holacracy/ (accessed: 1 October 2019).

So before implementing a self-management practice, it's imperative that all workers have elected to climb aboard: Gill, '10 components that successfully abolished hierarchy.'

It's possible, heck it's even wonderful, to see discipline invoked in such a way as to free and empower people: Ton, *The Good Jobs Strategy.*

Investing in people in this fashion leads to high performance: *Ibid,* p. ix.

In other words, 'being your best' and doing work that matters only holds weight when the goal of the company is worthy: *Teal Organizations Reinventing Organizations Wiki*. Available at: http://www.reinventingorganizationswiki .com/Teal_Organizations (accessed: 1 October 2019).

In 2016, Black Duck Open Hub, which tracks open source projects, reported nearly 4 million contributors working on nearly 700,000 projects: 'Open Hub' (2018) *Wikipedia*. Available at: https://en.wikipedia.org/w/index.php? title=Open_Hub&oldid=875128285 (accessed: 1 October 2019).

Together, by rehearsing and refining these practices, we refuse to cheat the world of our best contributions: https://www.amazon.com/War-Art-Through-Creative-Battles/dp/1936891026

12. Back to School Without the Bull

Riding on the coat-tails of the local startup scene, their big idea was to pitch East London as *Tech City*—a future startup mecca: *Tech Nation – The UK network for ambitious tech entrepreneurs Tech Nation*. Available at: https:// technation.io/ (accessed: 1 October 2019).

Shockingly, only one quarter of American employees believe in the values of their company: Dvorak, N. and Nelson, B. (2016) 'Few employees believe in their company's values', *Gallup.com*. Available at: https://news.gallup .com/businessjournal/195491/few-employees-believe-company-values.aspx (accessed: 1 October 2019).

Most notable is its emphasis on playfulness and collaboration while still catering to other modalities of work: *Financial Times* (2015) *Lucy Kellaway's Office Space: LEGO*. Available at: https://www.youtube.com/watch? v=GafKlghdB5Q (accessed: 1 October 2019); 'Case study: What is activity based working?' (2016) *SOFAble*, 30 May. Available at: http://www.sofable .eu/blog/case-study-what-is-activity-based-working (accessed: 1 October 2019).

Featuring a series of five distinct rooms, each is dedicated to a specific mode of work: the gallery for inspiration, the salon for conversation, the library for research, the office for light work, and my personal favourite, the chamber for deep work: 'How Cal Newport's deep work concept will influence office design – modern office furniture' (2016) *Strong Project*, 28 January. Available at: https://blog.strongproject.com/how-cal-newports-deep-work-concept-will-influence-office-design/ (accessed: 1 October 2019); Singh, A. (2018) 'You're working in the wrong place', *Medium*. Available at: https://medium.com/s/please-advise/youre-working-in-the-wrong-place-e289036ee01c (accessed: 1 October 2019).

The best workspaces in the future will place the highest priority on focus—optimising for workers to concentrate, contemplate, collaborate, and create: Ryon, B. (2016) 'A spectrum of spaces', *Microsoft*. Available at: https://news .microsoft.com/features/a-spectrum-of-spaces/ (accessed: 1 October 2019).

Talk about efficiency: the business has under 1,200 employees yet astonishingly powers 35% of all sites on the web: 'Deep look Into the WordPress market share (2019)'. *Kinsta Managed WordPress Hosting*, kinsta.com/wordpress-market-share/ (accessed: 3 April 2020).

'There are companies that are finding new ways to work, that allow people to set their own hours, have more flexibility, live wherever they want in the world and they're going to attract the best people'.: 'One Way Ticket—The Digital Nomad Documentary.' One Way Ticket—The Digital Nomad Documentary, digitalnomaddocumentary.com/ (accessed: 3 April 2020).

They cap their departments at 150 people because, as humans, they found that this was the maximum number of stable relationships that can be maintained at any one time: W. L. Gore are known to pave 150 parking spots outside of a given factory and when they are full up they build another similar sized building with more spots. Our developed brains let us maintain 150 stable relationships at any one time. More on the Dunbar number as it relates to business and our social media ties: AFP (2016) '150 is the limit of real friends on Facebook', *ABC News*, 20 January. Available at: https://www .abc.net.au/news/science/2016-01-20/150-is-the-limit-of-real-facebook-friends/7101588 (accessed: 1 October 2019); Delaney, K. J. (2016) 'Something weird happens to companies when they hit 150 people', *Quartz*. Available at: https://qz.com/846530/something-weird-happens-to-companies-when-they-hit-150-people/ (accessed: 1 October 2019).

Military units are often capped at this magic number too—when lives are on the line, it's helpful if everyone knows each other's name: Delaney, 'Something weird happens to companies when they hit 150 people'.

13. Tools to Help You Succeed

For many, the weekend is the most productive and creatively rewarding time, largely indistinguishable from the workweek: Boyer, B. (2015) 'Bye bye, Busytown', *Medium*, 30 June. Available at: https://medium.com/dashmarshall/bye-bye-busytown-f9b31c7d0abf (accessed: 1 October 2019).

Swedish psychologist K. Anders Ericsson, best known for his research on experts, found that what separates stand-out musicians, artists, chess players, and others is not just how long and hard they practise—but *how* they train: Ericsson, K., Krampe, R., and Tesch-Roemer, C. (1993) 'The role of deliberate practice in the acquisition of expert performance', *Psychological Review*, 100, pp. 363–406. doi: 10.1037//0033-295X.100.3.363; Stulberg, B. (2017) 'To get better at time management, borrow a training strategy from elite athletes', *The Cut*, 25 May. Available at: https://www.thecut.com/article/high-intensity-interval-training-work-productivity-breaks.html (accessed: 1 October 2019).

You might think you're an early bird or night owl but it's more than likely you're somewhere in the middle—a third bird: Pink, D. H. (2019) *When: The Scientific Secrets of Perfect Timing*. Reprint edition. New York: Riverhead Books.

This means you'll experience those dreaded afternoon dips sometime between 2 and 3 pm: Thompson, D. (2018) *Who Lives Longer – Night Owls or Early Birds?*, *WebMD*. Available at: https://www.webmd.com/sleep-disorders/news/20180412/who-lives-longer----night-owls-or-early-birds (accessed: 2 October 2019).

This is part of the reason why we do some of our very best thinking in the shower: The Editors of Time (2018) 'TIME The Science of Creativity', *Time*, p. 14.

It's simple, it's powerful, and even Navy Seals do it to chill out: 'The Navy SEALs breathing technique to calm down', *Examined Existence*. Available at: https://examinedexistence.com/the-navy-seal-breathing-technique-to-calm-down/ (accessed: 2 October 2019).

'Meditation is by far the most straightforward way to improve your concentration: a few minutes a day with your eyes closed, paying attention to the sensations of the breath in the nostrils, is the attentional equivalent of a decent workout at the gym': Burkeman, O. (2016) 'Why time management is ruining our lives', *The Guardian*, 22 December. Available at: https://www.theguardian.com/technology/2016/dec/22/why-time-management-is-ruining-our-lives (accessed: 2 October 2019).

You find that the problems that once had you stuck do so no longer: Oppezzo, M. and Schwartz, D. (2014) 'Give your ideas some legs: the positive effect of walking on creative thinking', *Journal of Experimental Psychology. Learning, Memory, and Cognition*, 40(4), pp. 1142–1152. doi: 10.1037/a0036577.

Bursts last around 52 minutes and rest periods about 17-minutes: Gifford, J. (2014) *The Rule of 52 and 17: It's Random, But it Ups Your Productivity*, *The Muse*. Available at: https://www.themuse.com/advice/the-rule-of-52-and-17-its-random-but-it-ups-your-productivity (accessed: 1 October 2019).

He required absolute silence with nine particular objects on his window-facing desk, including a vase of fresh flowers, a gilt leaf with a rabbit perched upon it, and a bronze statuette of a gentleman embracing a swarm of puppies: O'Kane, R. (2016) 'What would Dickens do? The rituals and routines of famous writers', *Writers Domain*, 27 June. Available at: http://blog.writersdomain.net/what-would-dickens-do-the-rituals-and-routines-of-famous-writers/ (accessed: 1 October 2019).

Some of the most prolific creators carefully limit both the frequency and the time they spend doing email: Gayle, A. (2016) 'CM 055: Jocelyn Glei on slaying the email dragon', *Gayle Allen*, 26 September. Available at:

https://www.gayleallen.net/cm-055-jocelyn-glei-on-slaying-the-email-dragon/ (accessed: 1 October 2019).

If you're a typical office worker, by bedtime, you'll have processed 124 emails: Glei, J. K. (2016) *Unsubscribe: How to Kill Email Anxiety, Avoid Distractions, and Get Real Work Done.* 1st edition. New York: Public Affairs; The Radicati Group (2019) *Email Statistics Report, 2015 2019.* Palo Alto, CA: The Radicati Group, Inc. Available at: http://www.radicati.com/wp/wp-content/uploads/2015/02/Email-Statistics-Report-2015-2019-Executive-Summary.pdf.

On average, finding an email by searching happens 41 seconds faster than trying to dig it out from a folder: Macpherson, S. (2011) 'Tip: want to be more productive? don't file your email – the latest on accounting tech for future focused firms', *Digital First.* Available at: https://digitalfirst.com/tip-want-to-be-more-productive-dont-file-your-email/ (accessed: 2 October 2019).

Of American smartphone users aged 18–44, 80% check their device first thing in the morning: Stad, A. (2013) '79% Of People 18–44 have their smartphones with them 22 hours a day [STUDY]', *Adweek 40.* Available at: https://www.adweek.com/digital/smartphones/ (accessed: 2 October 2019).

We should not let our smart devices outsmart us—like beautifully designed handcuffs providing endless opportunities to waste time: Fallon, S. (2015) 'The essential guide to happiness at work, with Rashida Jones', *Wired,* 23 June. Available at: https://www.wired.com/2015/06/rashida-jones-guide-to-happiness-at-work/ (accessed: 2 October 2019).

Five days a week, each morning at 7 am, he's in the same room, sitting in the same chair, tapping away on his same old trusty computer, and most importantly, with the same cup full of coffee: Newport, C. (2017) 'John Grisham's 15-hour workweek—study hacks', *Cal Newport,* 22 May. Available at: http://www.calnewport.com/blog/2017/05/22/john-grishams-15-hour-workweek/ (accessed: 1 October 2019).

One way to overcome all the noise is to set clear-eyed boundaries. In response to constant digital noise, some individuals temporarily quit social media while others, like Maneesh Sethi, go to crazy extremes—deliberately employing someone to slap him whenever he tries to check his Facebook

feed: Giang, V. (2012) 'This guy hired someone to slap him in the face every time he got on Facebook', *Business Insider*. Available at: https://www .businessinsider.com/this-guy-hired-someone-to-slap-him-in-the-face-every-time-he-got-on-facebook-2012-10 (accessed: 1 October 2019).

Glei also presents a compelling case for productivity where, from time to time, we should frankly just fuck off: Glei, J. K. (2015) 'How f*cking off can actually be quite productive', *Jocelyn K. Glei*, 4 September. Available at: https:// jkglei.com/how-fucking-off-can-actually-be-quite-productive/ (accessed: 1 October 2019).

When it gets to the nitty gritty, shapers consciously use technology as a tool, rather than a diversion: Bosker, B. (2016) 'The binge breaker', *The Atlantic*, November. Available at: https://www.theatlantic.com/magazine/archive/ 2016/11/the-binge-breaker/501122/ (accessed: 2 October 2019); Bulger, C. A. (2017) 'There's only one thing you need to have a sane relationship with your phone', *Quartz at Work*, 13 October. Available at: https://qz.com/work/ 1098750/mindfulness-is-the-key-to-using-your-phone-in-a-sane-way/ (accessed: 2 October 2019).

Computing power today enables us to complete the equivalent of a full 1970s workday in just one and a half hours: Krook, J. (2017) 'Whatever happened to the 15-hour workweek?', *The Conversation*. Available at: http:// theconversation.com/whatever-happened-to-the-15-hour-workweek-84781 (accessed: 1 October 2019).

Breakthroughs in microchip technology have caused productivity to more than triple since economist John Maynard Keynes predicted the shorter workweek nearly a hundred years ago. Surely he'd be rolling over in his grave to learn how ineptly we work and, more to the point, how we squander the precious time we could otherwise enjoy: Frase, *Four Futures*; Rifkin, *The Third Industrial Revolution*; Goldin, I. *et al.* (2019) *The Productivity Paradox: Reconciling Rapid Technological Change and Stagnating Productivity*. The Oxford Martin School. Available at: https://www.oxfordmartin.ox.ac .uk/publications/productivity-paradox-report/ (accessed: 1 October 2019); *BBC News* (2019) 'Stagnant productivity "costs workers £5,000 a year"', 5 July.

Available at: https://www.bbc.com/news/business-48885046 (accessed: 10 January 2020).

The average full-time American clocks 47 hours a week: Saad, G. (2014) 'The "40-hour" workweek is actually longer – by seven hours', *Gallup.com*. Available at: https://news.gallup.com/poll/175286/hour-workweek-actually-longer-seven-hours.aspx (accessed: 1 October 2019).

PART III: PRINCIPLES FOR THE FUTURE OF WORK

14. Learning: Wonder at Work

Education is what's done to you while learning is what you do to yourself. Ito and Howe, *Whiplash: How to Survive Our Faster Future*, p. 32.

Lyndon B. Johnson confessed, 'You don't learn anything when you're talking': Blitz, A. (2014) 'You don't learn anything when you're talking', *Accounting Today*, 21 July.

One inescapable truth of how we effectively learn is through imitation: This is really Behaviourism at work: modelling our actions based on our observable environmental conditions.

It's how we act and the stories we share that enable us to make progress: Rushkoff, D. (2019). *Team Human*. New York: W.W. Norton & Company; 'Time binding' (2011) *Wikipedia*. Available at: https://en.wikipedia.org/w/index.php?title=Time_binding&oldid=412208503 (accessed: 25 September 2019), p. 18.

They design kites to generate electricity and create next generation drones to deliver packages: *X – The Moonshot Factory X, the moonshot factory*. Available at: https://x.company (accessed: 25 September 2019); re:Work (2016) '"Culture Engineer" Astro Teller on failure and brilliance', *re:Work*, 20 July. Available at: https://rework.withgoogle.com/blog/astro-teller-on-failure-and-brilliance/ (accessed: 25 September 2019); Thompson, D. (2017) 'Google X and the science of radical creativity', *The Atlantic*, 10 October. Available at:

https://www.theatlantic.com/magazine/archive/2017/11/x-google-moonshot-factory/540648/ (accessed: 25 September 2019).

By effect, this permits the organisation to transform itself, according to systems scientist Peter Senge: Senge, P. M. (2006) *The Fifth Discipline: The Art & Practice of The Learning Organization.* Revised & Updated edition. New York: Doubleday.

Trumping that of any other workforce strategy is enabling workers to reskill, according to the World Economic Forum: Chan, S. (2019) 'World Economic Forum: Top 10 skills and workforce strategies in 2020', Human *Resources Online.* Available at: https://www.humanresourcesonline.net/world-economic-forum-on-the-top-10-skills-and-workforce-strategies-in-2020/ (accessed: 25 September 2019).

The work centred around synchronising, standardising, and maximising for productivity: See Toffler, *The Third Wave.*

'If you can't learn, you can't thrive': Newport, C. (2016) *Deep Work: Rules for Focused Success in a Distracted World.* 1 edition. New York: Grand Central Publishing.

This requires us to take ownership of our own means of production: Drucker, P. F. (1999) 'Knowledge-worker productivity: the biggest challenge', *California Management Review,* 41(2), pp. 79–94. doi: 10.2307/41165987.

The most valuable asset an organisation has is its people: Drucker, P. F. (1967) *The Effective Executive.* New York: Harper & Row.

We can catapult ahead when we learn how to learn how to change: Culatta, R. (2018) 'Experiential learning (Carl Rogers)', InstructionalDesign.org, 30 November. Available at: https://www.instructionaldesign.org/theories/experiential-learning/ (accessed: 25 September 2019).

Letting destructive behaviour fester, Tony Schwartz learned his lesson the hard way: Carter, S. B. (2012) 'Emotions are contagious – choose your company wisely', *Psychology Today,* 20 October. Available at: http://www.psychologytoday.com/blog/high-octane-women/201210/emotions-are-contagious-choose-your-company-wisely (accessed: 25 September 2019).

And if we fail to get to the root of the pain and the resulting behaviour, instead of a one-time kinda thing, it becomes chronic: Brown, B. (2018a) *Dare to Lead: Brave Work. Tough Conversations. Whole Hearts.* New York: Random House; Brown, B. (2018b) 'Leading from hurt versus leading from heart', *Brené Brown*, 4 December. Available at: https://brenebrown.com/blog/2018/12/04/leading-from-hurt-versus-leading-from-heart/ (accessed: 30 September 2019).

A whopping 60% said that their companies were not meeting a single one of those needs: Porath, C. (2014) 'Half of employees don't feel respected by their bosses', *Harvard Business Review*, 19 November. Available at: https://hbr.org/2014/11/half-of-employees-dont-feel-respected-by-their-bosses (accessed: 25 September 2019).

Everything comes down to the wolf we decide to feed: Zara (2016) 'The wolf I feed', *The White Noise Collective*, 2 February. Available at: https://www.conspireforchange.org/the-wolf-i-feed/ (accessed: 25 September 2019).

The wonder of their campus has made their *ways of working* the stuff of legend: Quinnell, J. (2018) 'LEGO – A guide to the perfect working environment?', *The Team*. Available at: https://www.theteam.co.uk/blog/workplace-design-lego-instructions-to-the-perfect-working-environment/ (accessed: 25 September 2019).

Sure, progressive schools that practice 'personalised learning' are numerous in Scandinavia: Shah, D. (2018) 'By The Numbers: MOOCs in 2018—Class Central', *Class Central's MOOC Report*, 11 December. Available at: https://www.classcentral.com/report/mooc-stats-2018/ (accessed: 25 September 2019).

This *banking* concept of education is wholly inadequate for capable learners in today's connected economy: Rose, M. (2017) 'The idea of the "banking concept in education"', *Our Politics*, 19 April. Available at: https://ourpolitics.net/the-idea-of-the-banking-concept-in-education/ (accessed: 25 September 2019).

Students need to be armed with growth mindsets, can-do attitudes, emotional intelligence, self-confidence, and the versatility to learn on the fly:

'Carol Dweck on creating a growth mindset in the workplace' (2016) *Farnam Street*, 16 November. Available at: https://fs.blog/2016/11/workplace-mindset/ (accessed: 25 September 2019).

But it's 'education that's meant to take us into this future that we can't grasp': Robinson, S. K. (2006) 'Do schools kill creativity?' Available at: https://www.ted.com/talks/ken_robinson_says_schools_kill_creativity (accessed: 25 September 2019).

It must build upon what we already know about intelligence, which is that it's diverse, dynamic, and distinct: *Ibid.*

15.　Feeling: An Emotional Revolution

After the Age of Enlightenment in the 18th century, we became enamoured with acting in the world: Harari, Y. N. (2014) 'Were we happier in the stone age?', *The Guardian*, 5 September. Available at: https://www.theguardian.com/books/2014/sep/05/were-we-happier-in-the-stone-age (accessed: 25 September 2019); Hy, K. (2017) 'Andrew Taggart (Ep.23): Skimming the surface of life', *RadReads*, 17 November. Available at: https://radreads.co/episode-23-andrew-taggart-b4d0b7ceb460/ (accessed: 25 September 2019).

And with our fixation on doing, comes the productivity ninjas and struggle pornographers we so cherish today: Eliason, N. (2019) 'No more "struggle porn"', *Medium*, 6 August. Available at: https://medium.com/@nateliason/no-more-struggle-porn-202153a01108 (accessed: 25 September 2019); Altman, J. (2018b) 'The 4-hour workday is not a crazy idea', *Quartz at Work*, 14 November. Available at: https://qz.com/work/1463545/the-4-hour-workday-is-not-a-crazy-idea/ (accessed: 25 September 2019).

We also know that beyond basic financial security, worker happiness doesn't increase with more pay and perks: We humanoids adapt with incredible speed to any newfound wealth. After about $75,000 in annual income per year, more earnings cease to have any significant impact on people's day to day happiness. Dunn, E. (2010) *Happiness and Money, Open Transcripts.*

Available at: http://opentranscripts.org/transcript/happiness-and-money/ (accessed: 25 September 2019); Dunn, E. and Norton, M. (2014) *Happy Money: The Science of Happier Spending*. Reprint edition. New York: Simon & Schuster.

Our feelings have also been assaulted by the advertising industrial complex for the better part of a century: *How One Man Manipulated All of America Freedom in Thought*. Available at: https://www.freedominthought .com/archive/the-man-who-manipulated-america-edward-bernays (accessed: 25 September 2019); Manson, M. (2019) *Everything Is F*cked: A Book About Hope*. New York, NY: Harper.

Charles Duhigg, a graduate himself, explains that the degree has been a far cry from a gilded highway to meaningful work: Duhigg, C. (2019) 'America's professional elite: wealthy, successful and miserable', *The New York Times*, 21 February. Available at: https://www.nytimes.com/interactive/ 2019/02/21/magazine/elite-professionals-jobs-happiness.html (accessed: 25 September 2019).

Half the working world are dissatisfied in their jobs while many others are *actively* **disengaged at work:** Levanon, G. (2017) 'Job satisfaction keeps getting better,' *The Conference Board*. Available at: https://www.conference-board.org/blog/postdetail.cfm?post=6391 (accessed: 25 September 2019).

Quietening the *shoulds* and enveloping the *musts*, shapers step up to create working lives we love: Luna, E. (2015) 'The crossroads of should and must', *Medium*, 19 May. Available at: https://medium.com/@elleluna/the-crossroads-of-should-and-must-90c75eb7c5b0 (accessed: 25 September 2019).

Erica Avey liked her job. But after microdosing LSD for six months, she quit: For Avey she was able to illuminate problems that existed beyond herself and made a conscious choice to ease these problems. Drugs may have aided her, but they do not need to be a part of the story. To learn more, seek professional guidance and take into consideration both your set (your mindset, physiological state, and the like) as well as your setting (where, with whom you do it.) Avey, E. (2019) 'Dosing after microdosing', *Medium*. Available at: https://medium.com/@ericaavey/the-long-term-effects-of-microdosing-lsd-b1d7103f645 (accessed: 25 September 2019).

Besides altering the *tripper's* sense of time, however, the jury is still out on this one: Rose, S. (2019) 'Do microdoses of LSD change your mind?', *Scientific American*, 16 April. Available at: https://www.scientificamerican.com/article/ do-microdoses-of-lsd-change-your-mind/ (accessed: 30 September 2019).

It's the conductor of our neural symphony and where our sense of self lives: Buckner, R. L., Andrews-Hanna, J. R., and Schacter, D. L. (2008) 'The brain's default network: anatomy, function, and relevance to disease', *Annals of the New York Academy of Sciences*, 1124, pp. 1–38. doi: 10.1196/annals.1440.011; Lieberman, M. D. (2013) *Social: Why Our Brains are Wired to Connect*. 1st edition. New York: Crown.

When volunteer psilocybin *trippers* were placed in an fMRI machine, activity in the DMN reduced: Chary, M. (2018) 'Psychedelic research finds ego exists in this part of the brain', *Gaia*, 13 July. Available at: https://www.gaia.com/ article/psychedelic-research-finds-ego-exists-in-the-default-mode-network (accessed: 25 September 2019).

It gives us the ability to understand and identify with the mental states of others: Rushkoff, *Team Human*.

If microdosing isn't your bag (and even if it is), the more popular and perennial means to melt the ego is through meditation: Garrison, K. A. *et al.* (2015) 'Meditation leads to reduced default mode network activity beyond an active task', *Cognitive, Affective & Behavioral Neuroscience*, 15(3), pp. 712–720. doi: 10.3758/s13415-015-0358-3.

Mindfulness doesn't affect work performance per se, but it sure as hell can lead to a loss in motivation: Altman, J. *Productivity Over Useless Posturing*, Jonas Altman. Available at: https://www.jonasaltman.com/writing/2018/ 12/31/productivity-over-useless-posturing (accessed: 25 September 2019) Hafenbrack, A. and Vohs, K. (2018) 'Mindfulness meditation impairs task motivation but not performance', *Organizational Behavior and Human Decision Processes*, 147. doi: 10.1016/j.obhdp.2018.05.001.

How we spend our time not working impacts how capable we are when we are working: Pang, A. S.-K. (2016) *Rest: Why You Get More Done When You Work Less*. 1st edition. New York: Basic Books.

Follow all that cognitively draining work you've done with deliberate rest: Recall K. Anders Ericsson, the psychologist we've encountered in Chapter 2 and his research on what makes for experts. Ericsson, Krampe and Tesch-Roemer, 'The role of deliberate practice in the acquisition of expert performance'.

If history is any indication, a bit of slacking really can be medicine for the soul: Pang, A. S.-K. (2017) 'Darwin was a slacker and you should be too', *Nautilus*, 30 March. Available at: http://nautil.us/issue/46/balance/darwin-was-a-slacker-and-you-should-be-too (accessed: 2 October 2019).

Research suggests that when you get busy (like real busy), your attention is hijacked: Mullainathan, S. and Shafir, E. (2013) *Scarcity: Why Having Too Little Means So Much*. New York: Times Books.

And while we may know the science-backed benefits of rest, most don't carve out nearly enough of this precious time: Seppälä, E. (2017) 'Happiness research shows the biggest obstacle to creativity is being too busy', *Quartz*. Available at: https://qz.com/978018/happiness-research-shows-the-biggest-obstacle-to-creativity-is-being-too-busy/ (accessed: 2 October 2019).

Every six years famed designer Stefan Sagmeister religiously decamps for his: Sagmeister, S. (2009) 'The power of time off' (TEDGlobal 2009). Available at: https://www.ted.com/talks/stefan_sagmeister_the_power_of_time_off (accessed: 2 October 2019).

This leads to better decision-making with a finer balance between objectivity and emotion: Gonzalez, M. (2014) 'Mindfulness for people who are too busy to meditate', *Harvard Business Review*, 31 March. Available at: https://hbr.org/2014/03/mindfulness-for-people-who-are-too-busy-to-meditate (accessed: 25 September 2019).

A heightened awareness of every sight, smell, touch, taste, and sound was essential for survival: Harari, 'Were we happier in the stone age?'

'The space and quiet that idleness provides is a necessary condition for standing back from life and seeing it whole, for making unexpected connections and waiting for the wild summer lightning strikes of inspiration – it is, paradoxically, necessary to getting any work done': Kreider, T. (2012) 'Anxiety: the "busy" trap', *The New York Times*, 1 July. Available at: https://query.nyti mes.com/gst/fullpage.html?res=940DEED8113AF932A35754C0A9649D8B63 (accessed: 2 October 2019).

'Boredom on the job was an incentive to creativity. I deliberately enter a period of boredom just prior to writing … because ultimately it brings me down to the centre of things from which all creativity comes': Pirsig, R. (2017) 'The motorcycle is yourself: Revisiting *Zen and the Art of Motorcycle Maintenance*', *CBC Radio*. Available at: https://www.cbc.ca/radio/ideas/ the-motorcycle-is-yourself-revisiting-zen-and-the-art-of-motorcycle- maintenance-1.2914205 (accessed: 2 October 2019).

The best moments of our lives often happen when we willingly stretch our minds to realise something that is both challenging and worthwhile: '8 ways to create flow according to Mihaly Csikszentmihalyi [TED Talk]'. *PositivePsychology.com*, March 12, 2020. https://positivepsychology.com/ mihaly-csikszentmihalyi-father-of-flow/.

'When one isn't dominated by feelings of separateness from what he's working on, then one can be said to "care" about what he's doing. That is what caring really is, a feeling of identification with what one's doing': Pirsig, R. 'The art of the skilled mechanic', *Awakin.org*. Available at: http://www.awakin .org//read/view.php?tid=452 (accessed: 2 October 2019).

Company cultures also need to provide crystal clear goals and embed mechanisms to make sure we're not just doing O.K. but also perpetually challenged: Spurlin, S. and Csikszentmihalyi, M. (2017) 'Will work ever be fun again?', in Fullagar, C. and Delle Fave, A. (eds) *Flow at Work: Measurement and Implications*. New York, NY: Routledge, pp. 182–195.

While there's no conclusive evidence that flow leads to greater productivity in the workplace, there is strong evidence that our perceptions, emotions, and motivation over the course of the workday are improved: *Ibid*.

Especially for those activities that require both spontaneity and creativity, being in a positive mood can impact our performance: Eisenberger, R., Malone, G. P., and Presson, W. D. (2016) *Optimizing Perceived Organizational Support to Enhance Employee Engagement*. Society for Human Resource Management and Society for Industrial; Organizational Psychology, p. 22. Available at: https://www.shrm.org/hr-today/trends-and-forecasting/special-reports-and-expert-views/Documents/SHRM-SIOP%20Perceived%20Organizational%20Support.pdf; George, J. and Brief, A. (1992) 'Feeling good-doing good: a conceptual analysis of the mood at work-organizational spontaneity relationship', *Psychological Bulletin*, 112(2), pp. 310–29. doi: 10.1037/0033-2909.112.2.310.

A professional life full of this deepness can be a truly satisfying one: Newport, *Deep Work*.

'I'm not going to progress in a linear fashion up the ladder of one organisation – assistant, manager, executive. My world of work, and how I work, looks very different': Cabraal and Basterfield, *Better Work Together*, p. 245.

We scurry to stay relevant. Indeed, the fear of becoming dispensable is a big trigger for shame: Brown, *Dare to Lead*.

And when the sense of making progress escapes us, we feel deflated: de Botton, *The Sorrows of Work*.

'As a result, we have seen a wave of professionals choosing alternative career paths or transitioning from traditional employment into freelancing, entrepreneurship, part-time work, or leaving the system altogether,' explains Gen Zer Francesca Pick and longstanding member of Enspiral Network: Cabraal and Basterfield, *Better Work Together*.

'Combining Romanticism and modern capitalism, as we are expected to do, is a near-impossible task': de Botton, A. (2018) *The Sorrows of Work*, 66.

'There is always a gap between achievement and desire. Feeling like a failure is the inevitable price for harbouring any sort of ambition': *Ibid.*, 98.

There's no time to waste, we can slay those stories that trap ourselves: Carey, B. (2019) 'Firing up the neural symphony', *The New York Times*, 14 May.

Available at: https://www.nytimes.com/2019/05/14/health/brain-memory-stimulation.html (accessed: 25 September 2019).

At least from time to time, we all want and maybe need to feel the ongoing WOW happening right now: Linklater, R. (2001) *Waking Life Movie Transcript.* Available at: https://wakinglifemovie.net/transcript/chapter/15/ (accessed: 25 September 2019).

Like it or not the future of work is emotional: Fosslien and Duffy, *No Hard Feelings*, p. 7.

16. Leading: Modes of Showing Up

Taylor, the oracle of time and motion studies, was stricken with insomnia, nightmares, and delirium: Goulder, B. W. (1969) 'The unemployed self', in Fraser, R. (ed.) *Work 2: Twenty Personal Accounts.* Harmondsworth, UK: Penguin, pp. 346–365.

His scientific management turned out to be a charade and, more to the point, the practices are wholly unfit for the work we do today: Stewart, M. (2006) 'The management myth', *The Atlantic*, 1 June. Available at: https://www.theatlantic.com/magazine/archive/2006/06/the-management-myth/304883/ (accessed: 25 September 2019).

We need different modes of leadership that are premised first and foremost on trust—more of an art than 'science': Altman, 'Four models for a modern leader.'

As celebrated four-star general Stanley McChrystal puts it: the interplay between leaders and their teams is a case of 'eyes on, hands off': Ryon, B. (2016) 'Leadership in transition', *Microsoft.* Available at: https://news.microsoft.com/features/leadership-in-transition/ (accessed: 25 September 2019).

And every leader was crystal clear on her most important task: to build great teams: McCord, 'How Netflix reinvented HR'; 'Humans hate being spun: how to practice radical honesty – from the woman who defined Netflix's culture' *First Round Review.* Available at: /review/humans-hate-being-spun-how-to-practice-radical-honesty-from-the-woman-who-defined-netflixs-culture/ (accessed: 25 September 2019).

When workers can reciprocally treat each other as competent professionals, they become accountable, empowered, and engaged: Zak, P. J. (2017) 'The neuroscience of trust', *Harvard Business Review*, 1 January. Available at: https://hbr.org/2017/01/the-neuroscience-of-trust (accessed: 25 September 2019).

'Leaders can let you fail, yet not let you be a failure': McChrystal, S. (2011) 'Listen, learn … then lead.' Available at: https://www.ted.com/talks/stanley_mcchrystal (accessed: 25 September 2019).

This catalytic learning ability first requires searching for new ideas, then integrating them, and finally using them to advance the organisation: Ready, D. A., Conger, J. A., and Hill, L. A. (2010) 'Are you a high potential?', *Harvard Business Review*, 1 June. Available at: https://hbr.org/2010/06/are-you-a-high-potential (accessed: 25 September 2019).

He decided to put all his chips on the table and focus on one thing: safety: Wilkinson, J. (2015) 'The power of keystone habits', *The Strategic CFO*, 29 July. Available at: https://strategiccfo.com/keystone-habits/ (accessed: 25 September 2019).

Including ways to boost efficiency and productivity: *Ibid.*

His management style is pretty darn simple: helping others succeed: Ghoshal, D. (2017) '"Let others succeed": Google CEO Sundar Pichai's simple but effective leadership style', *Quartz India*, 6 January. Available at: https://qz.com/india/879633/let-others-succeed-google-ceo-sundar-pichais-simple-but-effective-leadership-style/ (accessed: 25 September 2019).

'[Success] spreads and cascades': Popova, M. (2013) 'Givers, Takers, and Matchers: the surprising psychology of success', *Brain Pickings*, 10 April. Available at: https://www.brainpickings.org/2013/04/10/adam-grant-give-and-take/ (accessed: 25 September 2019).

In a world that has become increasingly interdependent, feminine values lay the foundation for our 21st-century operating system: Gerzema, J. (2012)

The Athena Doctrine (TEDxKC (2012)). Available at: https://www.youtube .com/watch?v=YxgTsyL4y0E (accessed: 17 March 2020).

Next Jump is the paragon of an inclusive culture where everyone is supported and elevated to be their best selves: Kegan, R. *et al.* (2016) *An Everyone Culture: Becoming a Deliberately Developmental Organization.* Boston, MA: Harvard Business Review Press. Next Jump is one of three companies globally that represent the future of work—what they call: Deliberately Developmental Organizations—the other two are investment firm Bridgewater Associates LLP and Decurion Corporation.

Using their own smarts to boost the intelligence of others they can make geniuses: Grant, A. (2014) *Give and Take: Why Helping Others Drives Our Success.* Reprint edition. Ottawa: Penguin Books, p. 63.

Companies with high degrees of trust surpass the average annualised returns of S&P 500 businesses by a factor of three: Covey, S. M. R. and Conant, D. R. (2016) 'The connection between employee trust and financial performance', *Harvard Business Review*, 18 July. Available at: https://hbr.org/2016/07/the-connection-between-employee-trust-and-financial-performance (accessed: 25 September 2019).

'Strategy emerges over time as intentions collide with and accommodate a changing reality': Rivera, G. (2012) *Emergent Strategy, Interaction Institute for Social Change.* Available at: https://interactioninstitute.org/emergent-strategy/ (accessed: 25 September 2019).

Nine out of every ten managers don't have what it takes to be great: Maurer, R. (2015) '1 in 10 have talent to be great manager', *SHRM.* Available at: https:// www.shrm.org/resourcesandtools/hr-topics/talent-acquisition/pages/talent-to-be-a-manager.aspx (accessed: 25 September 2019).

As organisational designers, they create psychologically safe environments for teams to be as fluid and effective as possible: Duhigg, C. (2016) 'What Google learned from its quest to build the perfect team', *The New York Times*, 25 February. Available at: https://www.nytimes.com/2016/02/28/ magazine/what-google-learned-from-its-quest-to-build-the-perfect-team .html (accessed: 25 September 2019).

These new modes of leadership are much more suited to the networked world we live in: 'Carol Dweck on creating a growth mindset in the workplace', *Farnam Street*.

17. Becoming: Our Social Fabric

And so it goes with our organisations that we build in our image: Leberecht, '4 ways to build a human company in the age of machines'.

'The system rewards and fosters those skills deemed useful and suppresses the expression of talents and faculties deemed useless, and thereby structures and imprints itself upon the individual personality and self': Goulder, 'The unemployed self', p. 348.

Think of the UX Designer/Disc Jockey/Yoga Instructor who is frowned upon by some and envied by others: Also known as multipotentialites. See Wapnick, E. (2015) 'Why some of us don't have one true calling' (TEDxBend). Available at: https://www.ted.com/talks/emilie_wapnick_why_some_of_us_don_t_have_one_true_calling (accessed: 14 January 2020).

No doubt, *becoming is better than being*: This 1960s saying was popularised by psychologist Carol Dweck in her book, *Mindset*. It alludes to those with fixed mindsets who don't allow themselves or to have the luxury of becoming since they prefer to stay as they are. Dweck, C. S. (2007) *Mindset: The New Psychology of Success*. New York: Ballantine Books, p. 25.

'The transhumanist movement is less a theory about the advancement of humanity than a simple evacuation plan ... but their ideas just extend our same blind addiction to consumption, destruction, progress, and colonization': Rushkoff, *Team Human*.

While 19th century wagon drivers became cabbies, many will not be so lucky and face a much gloomier fate: that of the superfluous horse: Raulff, U. (2017) *Farewell to the Horse: The Final Century of Our Relationship*. Translated by R. A. Kemp. London, UK: Allen Lane; Harari, Y. N. (2018) *21 Lessons for the 21st Century*. New York: Spiegel & Grau.

Many won't be exploited but will become something much worse: irrelevant: Harari, *21 Lessons for the 21st Century*.

But we have cleverer brains: Bostrom, N. (2014) *Superintelligence: Paths, Dangers, Strategies*. New York, NY: Oxford University Press, p. v.

We know there are a host of intelligences: Vital, M. (2014) '9 types of intelligence – infographic', *Adioma*, 17 March. Available at: https://blog.adioma.com/9-types-of-intelligence-infographic/ (accessed: 14 January 2020).

As of 2009, developmental psychologist Howard Gardner offered another one (existential intelligence): 'Howard Gardner, Multiple Intelligences and Education'. *infedorg*. Accessed April 4, 2020. https://infed.org/mobi/howard-gardner-multiple-intelligences-and-education/.

Intelligence itself is not linear but something beautifully expansive: Kelly, K. (2017) 'The myth of a superhuman AI', *Wired*, 25 April. Available at: https://www.wired.com/2017/04/the-myth-of-a-superhuman-ai/ (accessed: 14 January 2020).

'Whatever futurists may speculate about the singularity, right now and for the foreseeable future it is human beings, not algorithms, who will decide whether technology will make our lives better or worse': Dellot, B., Mason, R., and Wallace-Stephens, F. (2019) 'The four futures of work: Coping with uncertainty in an age of radical technologies', *RSA*. Available at: https://www.thersa.org/globalassets/pdfs/reports/rsa_four-futures-of-work.pdf (accessed: 14 January 2020).

'If we are to achieve a richer culture, rich in contrasting values, we must recognize the whole gamut of human potentialities, and so weave a less arbitrary social fabric, one in which each diverse human gift will find a fitting place: Mead, *Sex and Temperament*, p. 300.

We determine if the pattern will be disrupted and if the fabric of human history will be ruptured: Ray Kurzweil believes that the singularity will occur by approximately 2045 and technological change will be so rapid and profound it; 'represents a rupture in the fabric of human history'. Kurzweil, R. (2004) 'The law of accelerating returns', in Teuscher, C. (ed.) *Alan Turing: Life* *and Legacy of a Great Thinker.* Berlin, Heidelberg: Springer, pp. 381–416. doi: 10.1007/978-3-662-05642-4_16.

18. Futuring: The Long View

In just the past four decades, the US economy has more than tripled from $6.31 trillion dollars to $19.02 trillion: *US Real GDP by Year.* Available at: https://www.multpl.com/us-gdp-inflation-adjusted/table/by-year (accessed: 14 January 2020).

While America was becoming more productive, real hourly wages stagnated and in some cases fell: Gould, E. (2015) '2014 continues a 35-year trend of broad-based wage stagnation', *Economic Policy Institute*, 19 February. Available at: https://www.epi.org/publication/stagnant-wages-in-2014/ (accessed: 14 January 2020).

The ratio of pay between the average worker and his or her boss skyrocketed from 22:1 to 271:1: Dignan, A. (2019) *Brave New Work: Are You Ready to Reinvent Your Organization?* New York: Portfolio, p. 34.

These same trends can be seen in other developing nations: ter Weel, B. (2012) *Loonongelijkheid in Nederland stijgt.* CPB Policy Brief 2012/06. Centraal Planbureau; Kiersz, A. (2014) 'Here are the most unequal countries in the world', *Business Insider.* Available at: https://www.businessinsider.com/gini-index-income-inequality-world-map-2014-11 (accessed: 1 February 2020); Bregman, R. (2017) *Utopia for Realists: How We Can Build the Ideal World.* New York: Little, Brown and Company, p. 191.

The 26 richest billionaires own the same value of assets as the 3.8 billion poorest people: Elliott, L. (2019) 'World's 26 richest people own as much as poorest 50%, says Oxfam', *The Guardian*, 21 January. Available at: https://www.theguardian.com/business/2019/jan/21/world-26-richest-people-own-as-much-as-poorest-50-per-cent-oxfam-report (accessed: 15 January 2020).

Leading economist Mariana Mazzucato explains that the social, economic, and political impacts of this wealth division are devastating: Mazzucato,

M. (2018) *The Value of Everything: Making and Taking in the Global Economy*. New York: PublicAffairs, p. 4.

'[S]uch a city should of necessity be not one, but two, a city of the rich and a city of the poor, dwelling together, and always plotting against one another': OECD (2015) 'How does income inequality affect our lives?', in *Income Inequality: The Gap between Rich and Poor*. Paris: OECD Publishing, pp. 63–77. Available at: https://www.oecd-ilibrary.org/social-issues-migration-health/income-inequality/how-does-income-inequality-affect-our-lives_9789264246010-6-en;jsessionid=x8NahEEjZoOGvcHIbFlq4hPk.ip-10-240-5-103 (accessed: 16 January 2020).

TFP has gone flat, as have overall living standards: Gould, '2014 continues a 35-year trend of broad-based wage stagnation'.

Economists continue to scratch their heads in bewilderment at what's become known as the 'productivity puzzle': Office for National Statistics (2015) 'What is the productivity puzzle?' Available at: https://www.ons.gov.uk/employmentandlabourmarket/peopleinwork/labourproductivity/articles/whatistheproductivitypuzzle/2015-07-07 (accessed: 16 January 2020); Phillips, M. (2016) 'After 150 years, the American productivity miracle is over', *Quartz*, 9 March. Available at: https://qz.com/633080/the-rise-and-fall-of-american-productivity-growth/ (accessed: 16 January 2020).

'We're poorer, working longer hours, and leaving a worse world for our grandchildren than we otherwise would be': Klein, E. (2016) 'Technology is changing how we live, but it needs to change how we work', *Vox.com*. Available at: https://www.vox.com/a/new-economy-future/technology-productivity (accessed: 16 January 2020).

Life expectancy in the US is declining, yet American hospitals are the best in the world: Devitt, M. (2018) 'CDC Data show US life expectancy continues to decline', *AAFP*. Available at: https://www.aafp.org/news/health-of-the-public/20181210lifeexpectdrop.html (accessed: 16 January 2020).

Millennials have had to endure the bleakest financial future of any generation in over a century: Hobbes, M. 'FML: Why millennials are facing the scariest financial future of any generation since the Great Depression', *The*

Huffington Post. Available at: http://highline.huffingtonpost.com/articles/en/poor-millennials/ (accessed: 16 January 2020).

While the amount of stuff the US makes continues to explode, American manufacturing employment has plummeted: American manufacturing has actually dropped by 27 percent in the past two decades. Guilford, G. (2018) 'The epic mistake about manufacturing that's cost Americans millions of jobs', *Quartz*, 3 May. Available at: https://qz.com/1269172/the-epic-mistake-about-manufacturing-thats-cost-americans-millions-of-jobs/ (accessed: 16 January 2020).

'The whole idea that [America] is moving towards lower employment is a myth. We've faked lower employment through extremely extractive, exploitative, polluting, and unsustainable business practices': Rushkoff, D. (2019) 'The colossal problem with universal basic income', *Big Think*. Available at: https://bigthink.com/videos/the-colossal-problem-with-universal-basic-income (accessed: 16 January 2020).

We shouldn't forget that what we consume governs what we produce, and this then determines the nature of the jobs we have on offer: de Botton, *The Sorrows of Work*, p. 46.

It's clear that the industrial age imperative for efficiency and the subsequent ways we organise, grow, and compete no longer serve us: We come together in business for organisational structure, economies of scale, and healthy competition. Yet a scan of the global economy demonstrates a far cry from fair competition, technology giants scaling faster than they can bear, and ways of organising that still suppress and alienate people.

The attention economy has a financial incentive to keep us in a state of individualised anxiety and an obligation to constantly be reacting and producing: Odell, J. (2019) *How to Do Nothing* (XOXO Festival (2019)). Available at: https://www.youtube.com/watch?v=dveUrpp6vs8 (accessed: 16 January 2020).

Might we be going about measuring productivity ass-backward?: Klein, E. (2016) 'Technology is changing how we live, but it needs to change how we work'.

We could follow New Zealand's lead and, instead of designing budgets strictly under an economic umbrella, recognise the impact on natural, social, human, and cultural capital: Walters, L. (2018) 'NZ Government to lead world in measuring success with wellbeing measures', *Stuff*. Available at: https://www.stuff.co.nz/national/politics/101066981/nz-government-to-lead-world-in-measuring-success-with-wellbeing-measures (accessed: 16 January 2020).

Indeed, we've become more productive as humans and consumers, but not necessarily as workers: From Interview With Tom Streithorst, December 2019.

The following month marked the hottest month ever recorded on our pale blue dot: Aljazeera (2019) 'Iraqi province records world record with the highest temperature', *Teller Report*. Available at: https://www.tellerreport.com/news/2019-06-09---iraqi-province-records-world-record-with-the-highest-temperature-.SJevwKv50V.html (accessed: 16 January 2020); National Oceanic and Atmospheric Administration (2019) 'July 2019 was hottest month on record for the planet', *NOAA*. Available at: https://www.noaa.gov/news/july-2019-was-hottest-month-on-record-for-planet (accessed: 16 January 2020).

A path where just a slight jump in temperature spells catastrophe: droughts, floods, extreme heat, and poverty for hundreds of millions: More specifically, climate scientists report that we have until 2030 for global warming to be kept to a maximum of 1.5°C. after which point just one half a degree will be devastating for hundreds of millions of people. Watts, J. (2018) 'We have 12 years to limit climate change catastrophe, warns UN', *The Guardian*, 8 October. Available at: https://www.theguardian.com/environment/2018/oct/08/global-warming-must-not-exceed-15c-warns-landmark-un-report (accessed: 16 January 2020).

Not only can this reduce our carbon footprint, it may also provide more opportunity to engage in our communities as conscientious workers, citizens, and neighbours: Frey, P. (2019) *The Ecological Limits of Work: On Carbon Emissions, Carbon Budgets and Working Time*. Hampshire: Autonomy.

Available at: http://www.socioeco.org/bdf_fiche-document-6687_en.html (accessed: 16 January 2020).

Paul Lafargue, the son-in-law of Karl Marx, proposed a three-hour workday and the 'necessity to be lazy' as far back as the late 1800s: This is a phrase borrowed from Paul Lafargue, a pioneer of the shorter work week, *Ibid.*

Around the same time, philosopher Bertrand Russell advocated for the four-hour workday in an essay for *Harper's Magazine*: Russell, B. (1932) 'In Praise of Idleness', *Harper's Magazine*, October. Available at: https://harpers .org/archive/1932/10/in-praise-of-idleness/ (accessed: 16 January 2020).

Microsoft completed the Work-Life Choice Challenge, which saw 2,300 workers take five Fridays off in a row without a pay cut. Productivity soared forty percent: Paul, K. (2019) 'Microsoft Japan tested a four-day work week and productivity jumped by 40%', *The Guardian*, 4 November. Available at: https://www.theguardian.com/technology/2019/nov/04/microsoft-japan-four-day-work-week-productivity (accessed: 16 January 2020).

But what also occurred is more nuanced: happier workers, more efficient meetings, reduced levels of fatigue, and an overall improvement in health: *Ibid.*

The benefits of working less also mean fewer sick days, cost savings, and better work/life balance: Webb, W. (2016) 'Would a four-day workweek be more productive?', *Chief Learning Officer – CLO Media*, 31 August. Available at: https://www.chieflearningofficer.com/2016/08/31/a-four-day-workweek-more-productive/ (accessed: 16 January 2020).

With an improved sense of well-being and self-respect, workers tend to be more creative, committed, and collaborative: Veldhoven, M. van and Peccei, R. (eds) (2014) *Well-being and Performance at Work: The Role of Context.* Psychology Press; Schwartz, 'Rethinking Work'; Frey, *The Ecological Limits of Work.*

Autonomy, a UK-based Future of Work think tank, reports that a shorter workweek, amongst many benefits, also increases gender equality: Frey, *The Ecological Limits of Work.*

On the flipside, when we work overtime, it causes stress, anxiety, and sometimes depression: *Ibid.*

Scientific research has shown that the limit of our cognition is four-and-a-half hours of deep attention work per day, after which point we're kaput: https://psycnet.apa.org/record/1993-40718-001; https://qz.com/work/1463545/the-4-hour-workday-is-not-a-crazy-idea/

Our productivity wanes when we overwork, with some reports claiming that working over twenty-five hours per week makes you more stupid–especially for those over the age of 40: *Working more than 25 hours a week can make you stupid* (2016) *Advance Cessnock City*. Available at: https://advancecessnock.com.au/working-25-hours-week-can-make-stupid/ (accessed: 16 January 2020).

In Finland, teachers work some of the shortest workdays in the nation, allowing them to stay refreshed and engaged–a key contributor that makes their educational system one of the best in the world: Hemphill, A. (2018) *How teachers in the U.S. and Finland see their jobs.* Center for Public Education. Available at: https://www.nsba.org/-/media/NSBA/File/cpe-how-teachers-in-the-us-and-finland-see-their-jobs-report-july-2018.pdf?la=en&hash=8BB8003186563CA6873C8849F160400FE6049607; Nuffield Foundation (2019) 'Quarter of teachers in England report 60-hour working week', *Nuffield Foundation*, 18 September. Available at: https://www.nuffieldfoundation.org/news/quarter-of-teachers-in-england-report-60-hour-working-week/ (accessed: 16 January 2020).

At the time of writing, Finnish Prime Minister Sanna Marin has called for the entire country to move to a four-day workweek: Cheng, M. (2020) 'Finland's new prime minister wants her country on a four-day workweek', *Quartz at Work*, 6 January. Available at: https://qz.com/work/1780373/finlands-prime-minister-wants-her-country-on-a-four-day-workweek/ (accessed: 27 January 2020).

Meanwhile, the stress and burnout caused by overworking costs the UK economy billions every year: Arnold, S. 'Stressed economy, stressed society, stressed NHS', New *Economics Foundation*. Available at:

https://neweconomics.org/2018/05/stressed-economy-stressed-society-
stressed-nhs (accessed: 16 January 2020).

A shorter workweek means companies can reduce costs for items such as energy, electricity, food, commuting allowances, and variable office perks: DeFranco, L. (2018) 'Here's how much a four-day work week saves in expenses', *The Abacus Blog*, 23 August. Available at: https://blog.abacus .com/heres-how-much-a-4-day-work-week-saves-on-business-expenses/ (accessed: 16 January 2020).

And *less work* for some could actually mean freeing up more good work for others: Peyser, E. (2018) 'Every American should be working the same short hours as Trump', *Vice*, 9 January. Available at: https://www.vice.com/en_ us/article/gywwpq/every-american-should-be-working-the-same-short-hours-as-trump (accessed: 16 January 2020).

It means paying attention to your attention, not letting others rule your day, batching your work, and doing one task at a time: 'Working more than 25 hours a week can make you stupid'; Rodríguez, E. (2019) 'What would it take to get to a four-day work week?', *The Globe and Mail*, 26 November. Available at: https://www.theglobeandmail.com/business/careers/leadership/article-what-would-it-take-to-get-to-a-four-day-work-week/ (accessed: 16 January 2020).

If we get our act together, these tweaks could mean a new age of fulfilling work and a better way of life: Altman, 'The 4-hour workday is not a crazy idea'.

Employees may feel implicit pressure to work on days off or over weekends: We already see this behaviour at technology companies that haven't adopted a shorter workweek. Endlessly toiling away in lavish campuses, employees end up sporting golden handcuffs.

61% of UK workers think a four-day working week would make them more productive: Gough, O. (2017) 'Would a four-day working week really boost productivity?', *Growth Business*, 31 July. Available at: https://www .growthbusiness.co.uk/four-day-working-boost-productivity-2551710/ (accessed: 16 January 2020).

Secondly, UBI suffers from a terrible branding campaign: At the time of writing, 2020 presidential candidate's freedom dividend with news outlets dubbing him the $1000-a-month guy.

'Ration card that gives you access to all that is scarce in the world': Frase, P. (2016) *Four Futures*, p. 113.

'My hope is that we will follow our dreams instead of being stuck in dead-end jobs that rot our souls': Tom Streithorst, https://lareviewofbooks.org/article/a-new-golden-age-part-iii-the-basic-income-guarantee/ (accessed 3 March 2020).

Each family of four, all considered poor, got what today would be equivalent to $19,000 a year: Bregman, *Utopia for Realists*, p. 35.

Other trials in America, England, Kenya, Uganda, Brazil, Namibia, India, Finland, Italy, and the Netherlands show promising results: Lant, K. 'Universal Basic Income: UBI pilot programs around the world', *Futurism*. Available at: https://futurism.com/images/universal-basic-income-ubi-pilot-programs-around-the-world (accessed: 16 January 2020).

These innovative schemes can improve health and school attendance, reduce crime, and enable countries to become increasingly self-sustaining: Frase, *Four Futures*, p. 146.

The industry sees more finger amputations than any other in the nation. And bathroom breaks are often forbidden, forcing many workers to resort to diapers instead: Dispatches-Channel 4 (2019) 'Dispatches: Inside the "dehumanising" US poultry industry'. Available at: https://www.facebook.com/watch/?v=2403609706584045 (accessed: 16 January 2020); Guardian News (2019) Rutger Bregman tells Davos to talk about tax: 'This is not rocket science'. Available at: https://www.youtube.com/watch?v=P8ijiLqfXP0 (accessed: 16 January 2020).

To entertain a post-work society (a world without jobs) likely means you're doing A-okay: Beckett, A. (2018) 'Post-work: the radical idea of a world without jobs', *The Guardian*, 19 January. Available at: https://www.theguardian.com/news/2018/jan/19/post-work-the-radical-idea-of-a-world-without-jobs (accessed: 16 January 2020).

Fruitful trials depend on how much money gets doled out, under what conditions, in what frequency, and how it connects to the entire welfare system: Coote, A. (2019) 'Universal basic income doesn't work. Let's boost the public realm instead', *The Guardian*, 6 May. Available at: https://www.theguardian.com/commentisfree/2019/may/06/universal-basic-income-public-realm-poverty-inequality (accessed: 16 January 2020).

Current welfare systems are riddled with bureaucracy and see people in situations, like in the UK, where you may be better off if you don't work: Trashy British publications love touting the 'better off on benefits' story. There is much contention here because 'better off' is subjective. A single bachelor or even family may be more content on the dole and living on a shoestring. It's the quality of jobs on hand, which can be less than alluring, that must be taken into account. Financially, however, recent studies have calculated that one is better off working than not: Goulden, Chris. 'Yes, you're (still) better off working than on benefits.' *JRF*, 8 January 2018, www.jrf.org.uk/blog/yes-youre-still-better-working-benefits.

The company has double–downed on regenerative farming, perhaps the most effective way to store more water and draw more carbon out of the atmosphere: Marcario, R. (2018) 'Regenerative organic certification unveiled', *The Cleanest Line*, 12 March. Available at: https://www.patagonia.com/blog/2018/03/regenerative-organic-certification-unveiled/ (accessed: 16 January 2020).

But if we don't keep matters in check–whether that be companies scaling too fast for their own good, continued credit default swaps, or big tech takeovers–both the efficiency of the market and our freedom will continue to be under siege: Taylor, C. (1998) *The Malaise of Modernity*. Concord, Ont: House of Anansi Press, p. 100.

Our social inequality, economic stagnation, and financial instability might not be enough discomfort to spur a revolution: Streeck, W. (2016) *How Will Capitalism End?: Essays on a Failing System*. London: Verso.

It's reflected in our cultural melting pot, art that pushes the envelope, and efforts to solve our most pressing human problems: Hallmarks of The Renaissance were individualism, secularism, and humanism. Perhaps the new hallmarks of ours will be collectivism, workism (or spiritualism), and environmentalism.

The 2008 financial crisis presented an opportunity to course-correct that we squandered: 'Fiscal policy works by creating jobs and thereby putting money into the wallets of workers. Monetary policy works by raising asset prices, putting money into the pockets of rich people. Since 2007, policy makers have used ever more unconventional monetary policies, such as quantitative easing, to keep the economy from collapsing. What we should have done is shifted back to straight up conventional fiscal policy, investing in our future, improving our infrastructure, education and health care, creating jobs now, raising workers' wages and thereby creating the demand the economy craves.' From Interview With Tom Streithorst, December 2019.

And if words can alter how people see things, then things can change: Handy, C. (1984) *Future of Work: A Guide to a Changing Society*. Oxford: John Wiley & Sons, p. 185.

With an infinite number of futures ahead, we could lump them into the plausible, probable, and preferable: Kolehmainen, I. (2016) 'Speculative design: A design niche or a new tool for government innovation?', *nesta*. Available at: https://www.nesta.org.uk/blog/speculative-design-a-design-niche-or-a-new-tool-for-government-innovation/ (accessed: 16 January 2020).

'If we don't have a shared understanding of language then we are trapped in a default future'.: Remarks Lisa Gill founder of Reimaginaire inspired by the following passage: 'Language is the means through which your future is already written. It is also the means through which it can be rewritten…the unsaid and communicated without awareness… puts this part of language outside our control. Until we find leverage on this part of language, the future is written and can't be altered'. From: Zaffron, Steve, and David Logan. *The Three Laws of Performance: Rewriting the Future of Your Organization and Your Life*. Newick: Read How You Want, 2019.

'We might ease human misery but the battle can't be won – even as real progress is being made, the goal continues to recede': Gardner, J. W. (1971)

Self Renewal: the Individual and the Innovative Society. New York: Harper Collins, p. 98.

It's in these times of dissonance that mark the turning points of our collective future: Dani Shapiro, Still writing, p. 137.

In the new vista, work is meted out based on both fitness (current skills and capabilities) and needs (future capacities and proper value creation): Ondich, J. (2018) 'Bertrand Russell – two essays', in *Words of Wisdom: Intro to Philosophy*. Lake Superior College, Duluth, Minnesota: Jody Ondich. Available at: https://mlpp.pressbooks.pub/introphil/chapter/bertrand-russell/ (accessed: 16 January 2020).

We need to concern ourselves not with what could be, but what should be: See social philosopher André Gorz from Frase, *Four Futures*, p. 51.

As shapers, we present our best selves in everyday life: Gershon, 'How work changed to make us all passionate quitters'.

CONCLUSION: THE SHAPERS LEGACY

We act upon our free will not from a place of fear and anxiety but from strength and fullness: Taylor, *The Malaise of Modernity*.

Nearly all the world's population growth is taking place in less developed countries, and it's there where the possibilities for work must be created: Breene, K. (2016) 'What is the future of work?', *World Economic Forum*. Available at: https://www.weforum.org/agenda/2016/01/what-is-the-future-of-work/ (accessed: 16 January 2020).

GLOSSARY
OF WORK TERMS

Burst Working Intermittent and intense sessions of work with a high degree of focus and a 100% 'do not disturb' mode. See Deep Work

Deep Work Cognitively demanding and creatively rewarding work performed distraction free for up to two hours at a time. See Burst Working

Fluidity The ability to move quickly and with dexterity among constant change

Golden Hours Those periods of the day that you work at your very best, typically influenced by your chronotype

Great Migration The tsunami of workers that have and continue to strike out on their own and by and large adopting the Shaper mindset

Job Compensated or waged activities formally provided to an employer. The market determines financial compensation. Features a psychological contract and a veil of security

Meaningful Work Those activities that allow us to generate delight for ourselves by positively impacting another's life or by reducing their suffering

Perspective-Hacking The rapid ability to change the way you look at things through a range of practices including high-contrast conversations, meditation and travel

Shadow Talking Not saying what you think and then going behind people's backs and kvetching to colleagues

Shapers Individuals who deliberately shape their working life on a continual basis with the aim of feeding their soul

Work Deliberate activities engaged to achieve a goal of subjective significance. May or may not be compensated. A contract is not necessary, only the requisite motivation and resilience to accomplish something for the self and the greater good

ACKNOWLEDGEMENTS

Like the expression 'it takes a village to raise a child', I have now discovered that it also takes a village to write a book. While the experiences I've lived have culminated in what you hold in your hands, it's the people I've encountered along the way who have provided its texture. And there are simply way too many to thank here without surely putting you to sleep.

Teachers, thinkers, writers, mentors, colleagues, therapists, coaches, founders, friends, and family have all been instrumental in shaping my way of thinking. I'm especially indebted to those who were generous with their time to be interviewed for this book, participate in workshops, and provide invaluable feedback. You know who you are. In a road less travelled, you've guided me to see the horizon when there was nothing but fog. Thank you.

And to those who call me on my own bullshit and provoke me to live as if nothing stands in my way—while I hate and love you in equal measure—I do appreciate your candour.

Joel Altman is a bona fide DJ with words and the person who gives colour to the thoughts lodged in my head. Lynne Altman continually feeds my curiosity. And Aren Altman empowers me to live the shaper's life through his unwavering support. Thank you.

And finally to you, for picking up this book and giving your attention and time. For this I am eternally grateful.

ABOUT THE AUTHOR

Jonas Altman is a speaker, writer, and entrepreneur on a mission to make the world of work more human. As the founder of design practice Social Fabric, he creates learning experiences to elevate and grow leaders at the world's boldest organisations. His chronicles have appeared in *The Guardian, Quartz, The Telegraph,* and *The Sunday Times.*

INDEX